WALKING AND TREKKING ON CORFU

WALKING AND TREKKING ON CORFU

THE CORFU TRAIL AND 22 DAY-WALKS

by Gillian Price

JUNIPER HOUSE, MURLEY MOSS,
OXENHOLME ROAD, KENDAL, CUMBRIA LA9 7RL
www.cicerone.co.uk

© Gillian Price 2015
First edition 2015
ISBN: 978 1 85284 795 1
Reprinted in 2018, 2022, 2024 (with updates)

Printed in Singapore by KHL Printing on responsibly sourced paper .
A catalogue record for this book is available from the British Library.
Maps by Nicola Regine.
All photographs are by the author unless otherwise stated.

Thanks to my dear Nicola for taking me to this 'brilliant speck of an island in the Ionian' (L Durrell) – and for drawing his lovely maps.

Updates to this Guide

While every effort is made by our authors to ensure the accuracy of guidebooks as they go to print, changes can occur during the lifetime of an edition. Any updates that we know of for this guide will be on the Cicerone website (www.cicerone.co.uk/795/updates), so please check before planning your trip. We also advise that you check information about such things as transport, accommodation and shops locally. Even rights of way can be altered over time. We are always grateful for information about any discrepancies between a guidebook and the facts on the ground, sent by email to updates@cicerone.co.uk.

Register your book: To sign up to receive free updates, special offers and GPX files where available, create a Cicerone account and register your purchase via the 'My Account' tab at www.cicerone.co.uk.

Front cover: Breathtaking views down Corfu's south coast from the Agios Georgios ridge (Walk 13)

CONTENTS

Map key

——— sealed road	～ river, stream	P car park
——— lane	● village	† church, shrine, chapel
——— walk route	♖ castle, tower	🚌 bus stop
- - - walk variant	☼ belvedere	▲ mountain peak
(SF) start/finish point	⬆ accommodation	② walk number
(S) start point	✕ meals, refreshments	✈ airport
(F) finish point		

The inviting beach at Porto Timoni (Walk 8)

The old kalderimi track starts dramatically
(Corfu Trail, Stage 7 and Walk 9)

INTRODUCTION

Corcyra is all Venetian blue and gold
– and utterly spoilt
by the sun.
Lawrence Durrell, Prospero's Cell

To this description add brilliant wildflowers, lush countryside, quiet mountain villages, an agreeable climate, golden sand beaches, turquoise sea and breathtaking coastlines – and don't overlook affordable prices. Nowadays, famed Corfu – once known as Corcyra – is still a most desirable Greek island, as borne out by visitor numbers: all the languages of Europe can be heard in its hotels.

Brits in particular have been flocking here since Victorian times: many have stayed on, and over 10,000 now call the island their home.

Set at the bottom of the Adriatic, to the east of the 'heel spur' of Italy, Corfu is the northernmost of the beautiful string of Ionian islands. On the map Corfu resembles the stocky rear leg of a horse, kicking away from the mainland a matter of kilometres off the coast of Albania and Greece. The island's perimeter measures 217km, the surface area is 580sq km, and it stretches 62km from north to south.

Corfu is often associated with coastlines desecrated in the name of low cost package holidaying. Yet despite some construction sprawl – thankfully limited to a handful of resorts on the east and north coast and easily avoided – Corfu has much to offer the nature lover and walker. Many localities, including the island's interior, have escaped development altogether and retain a laid-back, traditional atmosphere. Moreover Corfu is the greenest of all the Greek islands and, with mile upon mile of paths and lanes, makes a superb destination for a walking holiday. Last, but definitely not least, the Corfiot people are amiable and helpful. In a nutshell, Corfu never fails to enchant.

As is the fate of islands, Corfu has had a chequered history. Famous figures have been visiting the island since antiquity: the ancient Greek hero Hercules (before he set out on his 10 labours), the Argonauts (after they got hold of the Golden Fleece) and Ulysses (who procured a ship to take him back to Ithaca). Rather later on came the Venetians – who stayed for close on four centuries (from 1401 to 1797). Under them Corfu – in view of its position perilously close to the huge Ottoman Empire – became a heavily fortified outpost. Despite a number of touch-and-go battles the island didn't succumb. Intermediate periods saw mainly French and British control: it wasn't until 1864 that

Old Venetian fort at Corfu Town

Corfu was finally unified with modern Greece.

The list of VIPs associated with the island includes European royalty such as Empress Sissi of Austria. For the majority of English-language readers Corfu is inextricably linked with the Durrell family thanks to the books of the brothers Gerald and Lawrence, relating their sojourns of the 1930s, the best-known of which is Gerald's *My Family and Other Animals*. For the record, Roger Moore also came by – as James Bond, during the filming of the 1981 film *For Your Eyes Only*.

This guidebook presents a selection of 22 day walks, perfect to do from a hotel or rented accommodation. The routes have been chosen to give a taste of the many different landscapes on this marvellous island. It also describes the long-distance Corfu Trail which stretches the length of the island.

THE CORFU TRAIL

Suitable for both novices and experienced walkers, this marvellous 150km (93 mile) trek explores Corfu from toe to top – far south to far north – in 10 memorable day stages.

In this guidebook each stage ends at a village or beach location with meals and accommodation for an overnight stay, be that privately rented rooms, *taverna* (local restaurant) premises or hotels across the range. Local shops sell picnic supplies, and many cafés and tavernas

Corfu Trail waymark

can provide lunch en route as well. On several walks there are accommodation options at intermediate points, meaning that the route can be shortened. Naturally, rest days are also feasible – maybe at a beach. The island's bus and taxi network allows walkers to join or leave the route at multiple points, with easy access to Corfu Town.

The CT is described here as a south–north route. It would be tricky, although by no means impossible, to walk in the opposite direction; however waymarks can be hard to spot and the route description awkward to follow.

Several UK travel agencies arrange for guided holidays on sections of the Corfu Trail, booking middle and top-end accommodation along with daily luggage transport as well as transfers. However, savvy walkers can easily do it themselves with the help of this Guide.

The old path to Krini leads through shady olive groves (Corfu Trail, Stage 7)

PLANTS AND FLOWERS

Corfu is smothered with huge numbers of glorious Mediterranean blooms and aromatic plants throughout the spring and summer. The seashore alone is home to myriad wildflowers. Clumps of grey velvety cottonweed (*Otanthus maritimus*) grow on the seaward side of low sand dunes, their thick stems lined with masses of lightly serrated leaves and topped with tiny tufted yellow blooms. The bushy everlasting or curry plant (*Helichrysum*) has unassuming woolly flowers of a golden hue at the tip of slender stems punctuated with silvery needle-like leaves: these release a curry-like aroma when rubbed.

Dry terrain near the seashore is the perfect habitat of the monstrous giant agave, or century plant (*Agave americana*), which can grow as tall as seven metres. Originally from Mexico, its spiky blue-grey leaves are clustered in a rosette at the plant's base. Its impressive trademark candelabra-like flowers, which appear at the end of the agave's life, grow on stems reminiscent of gigantic asparagus, and appearing to have come straight out of a science fiction film.

That same terrain is shared with the prolific – and considerably shorter – sea squill (*Urginea maritima*). This has slender rod stems, the top parts of which are lined with white blooms. The leaves dry up around the base of

Clockwise from left: the sea daffodil is also known as the sea lily; brilliant poppies enjoy the proximity of water; rockrose has fragile papery petals

the plant but its most characteristic feature is its huge onion-like bulbs, which can weigh up to 2kg, and more often than not protrude above the ground. Because the bulb continues growing even after it has been uprooted, in olden times the plant was attributed with magical powers of regeneration. Still today people hang it in their houses at New Year to guarantee good health and luck for the inhabitants.

More like a lily, and sometimes confused with sea squill, is the beautiful showy sea daffodil (or sea lily) that grows in clumps. Its bulb is not usually visible and its large trumpet-shaped flowers appear a couple to each stem. The Latin name *Pancratium maritimum* derives from 'all powerful', probably in view of the plants' capacity to survive in extreme conditions such as dry salty sand, although it may also refer to the plant's medicinal properties.

A little further inland flourishing bushes of rockrose (*Cistus*) with pale pastel paper-fragile flowers enliven the maquis scrub. This habitat is shared with thick masses of headily perfumed broom that colour hillsides and send bees into a frenzy. Walkers with keen eyes will find clearings in light woodland to be the perfect breeding ground for tiny exquisite orchids: an estimated 36 types have been reported on Corfu. Outstanding examples are the early spider orchid (*Ophrys sphegodes*), the woodcock orchid (*Ophrys scolopa*) and unusual

autumn-flowering lady's tresses (*Spiranthes spirales*), with tiny white star blooms on a plaited stem.

Poppies are many and memorable: eye-catching yellow horned-poppies (*Glaucium flavum*) sprawl on beaches, and are easily recognisable for their long pointed seed pods. Brilliant crimson specimens of the common poppy (*Papaver rhoeas*), on the other hand, are found along streams, forming vivid carpets in olive groves. Inland rural settings are also the habitat for colourful lupins (*Lupinus*) that mostly come in blue.

A surprising number of flowers bloom as late as September: meadow saffron, cyclamens and the white blossom of the common myrtle (*Myrtus*), a typical Mediterranean shrub whose evergreen leaves contain an essential oil. It was named after a legendary maiden from ancient Greece, who was slain by a rival (male) gymnast and turned into this lovely bush. The curious strawberry tree is another late noteworthy: it bears its white bell flowers and fruit at varying stages of maturity at the same time. When ripe, the rough red balls taste like strawberries – if you ignore the lumpy bits. The second part of the Latin name *Arbutus unedo* means 'eat one', implying that one is sufficient!

Extensive oak forests once cloaked the hilly island, and were widely exploited by the Venetians who used the wood for shipbuilding. They were partially replaced

The giant agave is never far from the seafront

by extensive and profitable olive groves: the Venetians paid the farmers to plant them, and accepted taxes paid in oil. An estimated three million graceful olive trees now thrive on Corfu. In early spring tiny sprigs of round, creamy blooms appear between the tiny blue-green leaves. A story narrates that the island's patron saint, Spiridion, appeared in a vision forbidding people either to prune the trees or pick the fruit; this may explain the abandoned look of the majority of the groves (cutting down trees is still prohibited by law), but not the fact that each winter families painstakingly collect the tiny black olives and press them to make fragrant oil.

WILDLIFE

The island is not heaving with wildlife, but a number of delightful sightings are on the cards. The magic flickering of fireflies is hard to beat of a summer evening. Another treat are the 83 species of butterflies. Freshwater terrapins are not uncommon inland, in or near streams, while yellow-and-black tortoises may be heard moving around in the undergrowth. Exported as pets in the 1960s, nowadays they are thankfully protected.

Birds of prey, including the buzzard and kite, are at home on open mountain terrain, such as the Pandokratoras. In a more urbanised setting, astonishing numbers of swifts, swallows and house martins swarm over Corfu Town

A timid tortoise on the sand dunes

The vast wetlands at Lefkimmi are home to many birds (Walk 20)

in shrieking black clouds during from the month of March all the way through to mid-October, before they head for warmer climes.

The hoopoe is unforgettable and eye-catching, as it runs and bobs its way along the ground. Vaguely like a woodpecker, it has a showy crest of black-tipped, chestnut brown feathers and black-and-white striped wings.

Water birds include the occasional flock of flamingos, along with waders such as seagulls, herons, spoonbills, egrets and oystercatchers that can be spotted at the important wetland sites of Lake Andiniotissa, Lake Korission and the old salt pans at Lefkimmi.

Potential danger may come in the shape of the island's small venomous snakes, but sightings are rare. The asp viper (*Vipera aspis*) is a smallish cream–hazel-coloured snake with a broad triangular head, whereas the horned viper (*Vipera ammodytes*), as its name suggests, has a horn on its snout and is a lighter grey–brown, with wavy markings. These snakes only attack when threatened or surprised – they may be drowsy when soaking up the sun on a path, so give them time to slither away. Their poison acts slowly and very rarely is the bite fatal. In the unlikely event that you are bitten, contact emergency services immediately. The number of these snakes has diminished drastically over recent years due to the widespread use of pesticides and weed killers.

Harmless snakes include the grass snake and the slow worm, the latter related to lizards. These come in many shapes and colours: the best loved is the ingenious gecko, which hangs onto walls and ceiling with its marvellous sucker feet as it hunts for insects attracted to light sources.

GETTING THERE

The easiest and cheapest way to reach Corfu is by plane. There is a huge choice of flights from the UK as well as northern Europe and Scandinavia. Companies that serve the island include British Airways, Easyjet, Ryanair, Thomas Cook Airlines and Thomson Airways. The airport (www. corfu-airport.com) is only 3km from Corfu Town, and handy airport minibus transfers can be arranged through www.a2btransfers.com and www. holidaytaxis.com. Should you need it, a city bus (frequent service) stops a 15min walk away out on the main road.

It is unquestionably more romantic, if more long-winded, either to drive or to take a train to Italy's Adriatic coast, then catch a car ferry from either Ancona, Bari or Brindisi. These leisurely overnight voyages conclude at the Greek mainland port of Igoumenitsa, from where there are plenty of connecting ferries across the straits to Corfu Town or Lefkimmi. Direct ferries to Corfu have unfortunately been shouldered out by the more lucrative cruise ships.

Corfu ferry awaiting passengers at Igoumenitsa

LOCAL TRANSPORT

Two excellent capillary bus networks radiate out from Corfu Town and cover virtually every corner of the island. Be aware that heavy traffic in and around the town often causes delays, especially on rainy days. It's a good idea at the start of a holiday to pick up a copy of timetables from the main ticket offices in Corfu Town so you can plan your movements.

The Blue Buses run around Corfu Town and relatively close destinations such as the airport, Benitses and Pelekas (tel 26610 39859 www.astikoktelkerkyras.gr for timetables). Villages further afield, as far south as Kavos and north to Aharavi, are served by the Green Buses, which also do long-distance runs to Athens and Thessaloniki (www.ktelkerkyras.gr tel 26610 28927).

Otherwise there are the island's taxis. Services are plentiful right across the island and fares are reasonable. Ask your hotel or B&B to call one for you. Alfa Taxi (www.alfataxicorfu.net tel 26630 32400) covers the north of the island, as does the taxi company tel 26610 30180. For the south of the island call mob 6977 864823 (www.southcorfutaxi.com).

INFORMATION

The official Greek Tourist Authority website (www.visitgreece.gr) has all sorts of helpful and inspiring information about Corfu. There are currently no tourist offices on the island.

More walk suggestions can be found at www.zizyphus.co.uk.

WHEN TO GO

The best time to go is May–October, when everything is functioning and in full swing. Walking on the island is possible year-round, but much of the accommodation and restaurants closes down in late October and does not open again until late April/May. This is of crucial importance for walkers on the Corfu Trail. That said, in the off season it is not impossible to find hotels and flat owners prepared to let out premises even for a single night, and people are unfailingly helpful in finding walkers a place to stay.

The weather is the other determining factor. Corfu's climate is temperate, mild in winter and with sunny balmy days in summer, often tempered by a sea breeze. Maximum temperatures on Corfu are 23°C in May, 31°C July/August then 23°C in October. Midsummer, on the other hand (July–August in particular), is not the best time to walk low-level routes due to the scorching sun and hot winds, which can make long, shadeless stretches too warm and unpleasant. Moreover beach resorts and Corfu Town will be heaving. On the plus side, however, walks close to the coast can be followed up with a refreshing swim in the turquoise

The White House at Kalami (Walks 1 and 2)

Ionian Sea, which is at its warmest in August, when the water temperature averages 27°C. Winter spells storms and heavy rain, especially from November through to February, and snow can appear on the mountains (it is this precipitation that makes Corfu so lush and green.) The driest months are May–September.

ACCOMMODATION

For visitors planning day walks Corfu offers an excellent choice of reasonably priced hotels and family-run guesthouses, often with an attached café-restaurant. Some suggestions can be found in Appendix B. Staying in a resort, usually booked through a tour operator, can be an excellent deal thanks to the all-inclusive formula whereby limitless meals and drinks are paid for in advance, but check the location carefully. Unless you opt for accommodation in Corfu Town or a village with good bus links, a hire car will be essential to access the walks.

Hotels and resorts generally accept credit cards, but always check, especially at small family-run establishments. Where possible reserve in advance, either directly to the accommodation provider or online through

Corfu offers many family-run guesthouses, often with an attached café-restaurant

sites such as www.booking.com (which charge owners a commission). Rooms to let always have an en suite bathroom, and often turn out to be flats with a kitchen: at worst there will be an electric kettle. Breakfast is not always included, often an advantage for walkers who can see to their own and make an early start instead of wandering around a village in search of an early-opening café. Be aware that many apartments are available for single-night stays as well as longer term. Don't hesitate to ask.

The Corfiots are great gardeners and many hotels and rented rooms are pleasantly set amid scented lemon trees or flourishing flower and vegetable gardens.

A mix of private rooms and hotels can be found along the Corfu Trail: these are referred to in the stage descriptions as well as in Appendix B. Not all have a website or email address, so some phone calls will be necessary.

Camping is definitely an option for the Corfu Trail. Walkers suitably equipped and used to lugging around the extra weight will enjoy the freedom and versatility. Most villages en route have a small grocery shop. There are a couple of buts to wild camping on Corfu: finding water can

Lemon blossom and fruit

COMMUNICATIONS

If you don't have overseas coverage with your normal mobile phone provider, consider buying a Greek SIM card for those local calls. (You will need a photocopy of your passport for this.) This is especially important for Corfu Trail walkers who may need to phone day by day to arrange accommodation. Phone credit is easily purchased at newspaper kiosks and local shops.

These days the majority of hotels and rented rooms have WiFi.

be a problem, wandering livestock are not uncommon, and permission should always be requested before pitching a tent on private property.

FOOD AND DRINK

Flavoursome, simple and healthy is the best way to describe the food on Corfu. Expect plenty of locally grown vegetables, salads, meat and sometimes fish, all accompanied by the

Taverna at Agios Stefanos (Walk 7)

island's tasty olive oil. Ubiquitous unmissable classics include Greek salad – crunchy chunks of cucumber, tomato, green pepper and feta cheese with onion and black olives. Then there's *moussaka* – a baked pie of aubergine and minced meat topped with a thick white sauce and cheese. *Souvlaki* are grilled skewers of meat while *stifado*, *sofrito* and *pastitsada* are delicious home-style stews or casseroles with beef, veal or rabbit with onions and pasta. *Meze* refers to a snack such as a small plate of olives and cheese to accompany a glass of wine. Apart from the traditional crumbly feta cheese, made from sheep or goat's milk and stored in brine, cheeses tend to be mild.

For picnic lunches village cafés and shops will usually rustle up a sandwich or roll for you. It's a good idea to learn the Greek terms for bread, ham, cheese and so on (see Appendix C). Savoury pastries – such as *spanakopita* with spinach and feta or *tiropita* with cheeses – make a delicious lunch if you're lucky enough to find a good bakery.

Sweets are never lacking, especially in Corfu Town and larger villages that have a café-cum-cake shop. The mouth-watering array of Greek desserts includes the all-time favourite *baklava* – layers of flaky filo pastry and chopped nuts, drenched in honey. Luscious thick Greek yoghurt is a common dessert. Walkers will appreciate *pasteli* – bars of honey with sesame or almonds – as they travel well.

As regards drinks, locally brewed and bottled ginger beer, originally introduced by the British, is especially refreshing after a walk: freshly squeezed orange juice is another contender. *Portokalada* is orangeade and *lemonada* the lemon equivalent.

Red, white and rosé wines are available, many home grown or hailing from other regions of Greece. *Kumquacello* is a bright orange sweetish liquor made with the rind of kumquats. This tiny citrus fruit, resembling a smaller version of a mandarin, was introduced to Corfu from Southeast Asia in the 1860s.

Tap water is fine to drink, unless specified otherwise. Bottled water shipped in from the mainland is always on sale.

As in other parts of Greece, local restaurants are known as *tavernas* and they serve lunch and dinner. Rare is the village without a coffee shop, usually the exclusive realm of the menfolk who gather around a table to pass the time of day. Traditional Greek coffee is dense, short and sweet, made with ground coffee boiled with sugar: visitors are usually offered instant coffee or international styles in hotels and restaurants.

Be aware that tavernas, cafés and local shops tend to close between 2 or 3pm and 5.30pm, as many people take a siesta then.

WHAT TO TAKE

Give careful thought to gear for walking. Here are some suggestions:

- lightweight walking boots are essential for the Corfu Trail as well as for routes over rough ground with loose stones. They will help avoid twisted ankles and sore feet and are safer on wet and slippery terrain. Good trainers with thick soles are fine for shorter simpler routes. Apart from Walks 18 and 20 keep sandals for the beach as they can be downright dangerous on mountain paths
- a medium sized rucksack for the Corfu Trail, or a small day pack for the shorter walks
- long lightweight trousers protect legs from a scratching on overgrown paths
- T-shirts and shorts – remember that you'll often be walking through villages so avoid anything too revealing
- a light fleece
- a whistle, headlamp or torch for attracting help in an emergency: don't rely on your mobile phone as there is often no signal
- snack food such as dried fruit, *halva*, muesli or sesame bars on sale in village shops
- trekking poles are useful for the Corfu Trail
- rain and windproof gear such as lightweight jacket, rucksack cover and over-trousers
- sun protection – a hat, high factor sun cream and sunglasses
- a swimming costume and a lightweight towel or sarong come in handy on those coastal walks when you want to stop for a swim; a mask and snorkel are a boon for exploring the underwater realms

On a paved stretch of the 'Secret Path' (Walk 5)

- lightweight plastic sandals for walking on pebble beaches
- a compass for those places where waymarking is scarce and route directions need to be closely adhered to
- a water bottle
- a supply of tea bags or instant coffee and biscuits for a DIY breakfast
- a first aid kit including insect repellent, as mosquitoes can be a pest during the summer months. Also take something to deal with wasp or other insect bites: the island's chemists are well supplied.

MAPS AND PLACE NAMES

Sketch maps are provided with each walk in this Guide. Key landmarks and as much useful detail as possible have been crammed in, dictated by limits of space and graphics. In most cases these maps, along with the route description, are sufficient for the walks. However, it is always a good idea to get hold of a larger commercial map for many reasons: they are helpful when planning your trip, put places in a wider context, help you identify points of interest, and are essential in orientation if you lose your way.

The Anavasi 1:56,000 scale map is the best for walking. It is widely available on the island as well as online from www.anavasi.gr and at bookshops in the UK. For a glossary of commonly used geographical terms on maps and signs see Appendix C.

As can be expected, place names on Corfu are in Greek script, although many have been transcribed to English characters and often translated on signs to help visitors. However, there are huge variations in spelling. The versions in this Guide are based on those on the Freytag & Berndt map. Note that Corfu Town is also referred to as Kerkyra.

Another thing to watch out for is the recurrence of identical or very similar names. A common example is Pantokrator or Pandokratoras – Christ depicted as all-embracing, ruler of the universe, The Almighty. Numerous chapels bear his name, and have often given the name to the mountain they stand on. The only true Oros Pandokratoras (Mount Pandokratoras) is the highest point on Corfu in the

The Pantokrator, Christ the Almighty

SAINT SPIRIDION

Spiridion was a 4th-century Cretan shepherd who took his vows on the death of his wife and went on to become a bishop. He was credited with some miracles during his lifetime. When Crete was taken over by the Arabs his body – still intact – was moved to Constantinople. In 1453 a Corfiot monk took the embalmed remains to Corfu, where they are still held in great awe today and attributed with miraculous influence. Spiridion is known as the Keeper of the City for his help in expelling both the plague and the Turks – on that occasion he appeared in a vision to the invaders, threatening them with a cross and a flaming torch.

northeast. Others often referred to as Pantokrator for their eponymous monasteries are the Agii Deka massif between the villages of Agios Deka and Stavros, and Agios Mattheos further south.

Agios or *Ayios* – pronounced 'eye-eos' – means 'saint' (the term gave rise to 'hagiography', the lives of the saints, in English). An immensely popular place name is Agios Georgios (Saint George). There are two beach locations with this name – one in the north and the other in the south. For the purposes of this Guide, one is referred to as Agios Georgios south and its counterpart Agios Georgios north. To confuse things more, there's a Mount Agios Georgios on the west coast, not to mention the village of similarly spelled Agios Gordios to its south. Agios Georgios south is sometimes referred to as Agios Georgios Argyrades, and Agios Georgios north as Agios Georgios Pagi.

Spiridion is the island's highly revered patron saint: however, curiously few places have been named after him – apart from the place where the Corfu Trail concludes.

DOS AND DON'TS

When out walking on Corfu keep the following points in mind:

- allow plenty of extra time for wrong turns, fallen trees and mud after heavy rain: these can hamper progress
- carry all your rubbish away with you
- avoid treading on the nets in olive groves – they're expensive
- close all gates behind you
- don't light any fires and, if you smoke, put out cigarettes carefully as the vegetation can be as dry as tinder
- carry lots of water wherever you go walking: villages do not have drinking fountains and streams are often polluted by chemicals used in agriculture; refreshment points – cafés and the like – are

Avoid treading on the nets under olive trees

listed in the information box for each walk

- remember that people live here: stay on the paths and don't walk through private property
- walkers on the Corfu Trail should carry a good supply of euros in cash as unlike the larger hotels, small establishments don't usually accept credit cards and the only ATMs en route are at Kavos and Paleokastritsa
- don't expect everyone to speak English: find time to learn some Greek expressions (see Appendix C). This will endear you to the Corfiots.

EMERGENCIES

In case of emergency call:
- ambulance tel 166
- police tel 100.

USING THIS GUIDE

This Guide describes a selection of 22 shorter walks designed to fit into a single day. The majority are circuits with a return to the start point. They are listed under four chapters: northeast, northwest, centre and south. Each chapter begins with an introduction outlining the area's main features, villages and transport and accommodation facilities.

The Guide then describes the Corfu Trail (CT), which has been split up into 10 stages, each corresponding to a reasonable day's walking, and always concluding at a village where meals and accommodation can be found. Walkers with less than 10 days' holiday can slot in or bail out at the many villages linked by bus to Corfu Town. Handy places include Potami, Agios Georgios south, Pelekas and Agios Georgios north. Otherwise one of the island's reliable and reasonably priced taxis can be used.

Not many walking routes on Corfu are waymarked so the detailed route descriptions and maps in this guide need to be followed carefully.

Each stage for the CT and the day walks have an information box containing the following essential data:
- walk start and finish point
- distance (given in kilometres)
- ascent and descent: this is important information, as height gain and loss are an indication of effort required and need to be taken into account alongside difficulty and distance when planning the day
- difficulty – each walk has been classified by grade, although adverse weather conditions will make any route more arduous:
  - Grade 1 – an easy route on clear tracks and paths, suitable for beginners
  - Grade 2 – paths across hill and mountain terrain, with lots of ups and downs; a reasonable level of fitness is preferable
  - Grade 3 – strenuous, entailing prolonged ascent/

descent, possibly with orientation problems: experience and extra care are recommended

- walking time: this does not include time out for rests, picnics, views, photos or nature stops, so as a general rule double the walk times given when planning your day. Every walker goes at a different pace and makes an unpredictable number of stops along the way, so the 'skeleton' times given are a guide.

Compass bearings are abbreviated (N, S, NNW and so on). Reference landmarks and places encountered en route are in **bold type**. Altitudes are given in metres (m) above sea level (100m = 328ft).

The descent path below Old Perithia (Walk 3 and Corfu Trail, Stage 10)

Life in the island's northeast is lived in the shadow of the sprawling limestone massif of the Pandokratoras. Soaring to 911m above sea level, for the most part this is arid pasture land for wandering goats who can survive on thorny scrub. For walkers the rocky mountain means lengthy slogs across rugged terrain with little shade – but the upsides are solitude and huge views over the sparkling Ionian Sea to scattered islands and the mainland. The mountainsides slope down through dense woodland and extensive olive plantations to beautiful coastlines. To the east the sheltered coast juts out into the Straits of Corfu, mere kilometres from Albania. Thousands of escapees swam to Corfu or paddled across on tyre inner tubes in 1990, after communism in the country collapsed and its borders opened up. These days the shore is a string of enchantingly small, secluded coves with pebble beaches and inviting tavernas. It is a favourite with upmarket yachting types, which is sometimes reflected in accommodation and restaurant prices. The main coast road links Ipsos and Barbati with Kassiopi and Aharavi, and is served by buses throughout the summer months.

Walk 1 takes a stroll along the delightful coastal path that links up all the lovely bays between Kaminaki and Kerasia. Places with accommodation en route include Nissaki bay (sometimes referred to as Krouzeri beach), with apartments and a large multi-starred hotel. Kalami, on the other hand, is located a short way off the main coast road (15min on foot from the bus stop) and is a quiet place to stay. At one end of its beach stands an attractive landmark villa, The White House, former home of the writer Lawrence Durrell. Its other claim to fame is as the bay where Sir Timothy Havelock and his wife are assassinated in the Bond film *For Your Eyes Only*. Kalami is also the start point for Walk 2, a memorable circuit embracing both coast and mountain.

In surprising contrast is the northern coastline, with beautiful long sandy beaches flanked by low rocky headlands culminating in Cape Agia Ekaterinis, the northernmost point of Corfu, which encloses Lake Andiniotissa, a protected nature area and haven for birds and otters. The headland is explored in Walk 4 and

Kaminaki beach where the coastal path begins

the long-distance Corfu Trail concludes nearby.

Not far inland – 8km due south but 420m above sea level on the mountain's flank – is the atmospheric village of Old Perithia, reputedly a Byzantine settlement but in all probability much older. Only a handful of people call it home during summer, and they run local restaurants, cafés and a boutique B&B. The CT transits here, as does Walk 3.

Down at sea level, the sprawling township of Aharavi (also spelt Acharavi) makes a good base for the area, with plenty of shops, accommodation and year-round bus links with Corfu Town, not to mention a lovely 7km-long sandy beach. Walk 5 begins there.

WALK 1

Kaminaki to Kerasia coastal path

Start/Finish	Kaminaki
Distance	10.5km
Ascent/Descent	50m/50m
Grade	1–2
Walking time	3hr 30min (1hr 45min one-way)
Refreshments	Kaminaki, Nissaki bay, Agni, Kalami, Kouloura, Kerasia
Access	Kaminaki – and indeed all of the main beaches visited during the walk – are accessible by car, mostly down steep narrow roads off the main coastal artery. If you catch the bus (Kassiopi line), tell the driver you want to get off at the turnoff for Kaminaki; from the bus stop it's 15min on foot down to the waterfront where the walk starts – either follow the yellow Corfu Trail markers or take the road. At Kerasia, it's 2km up to the road and the bus stop, if you conclude the walk there

This divine wander along Corfu's rocky northeastern coast drops in at a string of pretty coves and bays. The mountainous Albanian mainland, only kilometres away across the straits, is a constant companion. Allow plenty of extra time, as you'll be constantly distracted by seafront eateries and inviting swimming spots. The main beaches have pebbles rather than sand and are equipped with the usual sun beds, umbrellas and laid-back tavernas, but walkers are likely to have the other coves all to themselves. Don't forget your swimming costume and sun protection. Most of the walk uses clear easy pathways, while a short stretch follows a quiet road. Trainers, not sandals, are recommended.

At charming **Kaminaki**, where the pebbly seafront is lined with tavernas, go L (NNE) to the end of the beach. Here a clear path leads along the rocky coast in the company of giant agave plants. Private secluded villas perched in scenic spots are passed. It's not far to **Nissaki bay**, which is popular with the groups at the only big hotel on this

Kassiopi
Agnitsini
Kerasia
Mengoulas
Porta
Chouchoulio
Kouloura
Kalami
White House
1
Gialiskari
Agni
Kentroma
Corfu Town
Nissaki bay
Kaminaki
SF
N
0
1
km

*On the following
section construction
work on new villas
may interfere with
the path. Be prepared
to detour. To be safe,
join the walk at Agni.*

stretch of coast. Continue past the swimming pool to the bar then go up left and along the front of the hotel building to where the lovely path resumes, as does peace and quiet. Shaded by olive trees and flanked by bleached rocks, the way soon climbs steeply albeit briefly on steps circling private property. ◄ Further along gradual descent concludes at lovely **Agni** beach. Here you walk through the premises of friendly Nikolas Taverna.

Once the jetty and other eateries have been passed you pick up the path once more, signed for Gialiskari beach. This climbs a little through holm oak wood on another lovely stretch leading to quiet **Gialiskari** beach, an expanse of pebbles in a secluded cove where yachts moor. Here fork left, following signs for Kalami. A wall of prickly pear shrubs and a vegetable plot are passed and it's up to join a concreted lane through olive groves. At a tarmac road, continue straight ahead in descent for the short distance separating you from the landmark villa the **White House**.

The former residence of expatriate British writer Lawrence Durrell, the cube-shaped **White House** is now a charming restaurant with accommodation.

Immediately after the building take the steps to the waterfront and jetty and proceed along the beach of **Kalami** (**1hr**) with its eateries.

The charming harbour at Kouloura

At the far end take the steps to the road and follow the tarmac up the hill to an intersection where you need the downhill fork for Kouloura. At the bottom you go right for the promontory housing highly photogenic **Kouloura**, with its petite harbour for fishing boats, taverna and 11th-century church.

Backtrack to the last turnoff and keep straight ahead to the beach of **Chouchoulio**, shaded by towering eucalyptus trees. Near an old building at the far end is a path signed for Kerasia. This leads around the next point to a quiet pebble beach which concludes at low cliffs. These are avoided as the path forks left for a lovely wander across the low headland. Just after another small beach ignore the turn-off left for overgrown 'Public path main road' and keep on the level way in the company of masses of white sea squills and thorny bushes. **Kerasia** beach (**45min**) is a lovely conclusion to the walk. ▸

The long quiet pebbly beach is backed with shady eucalypts, and there's a taverna at the far end.

Return the same way to **Kaminaki** (**1hr 45min**). Alternatively, if you want to call it a day here, look for the sign halfway along the beach pointing inland for a route leading up to the main road.

WALK 2
Kalami to Menegoulas loop

Start/Finish	Kalami
Distance	15km
Ascent/Descent	550m/550m
Grade	2–3
Walking time	5hr
Refreshments	Porta, Kaminaki, Nissaki bay, Agni, Kalami
Access	Kalami is 1.5km off the main coastal road: if you catch the bus (Kassiopi line), ask the driver where to get off; from the bus stop it's 20min on foot down to the waterfront where the walk starts

This is an excellent – if long and tiring – circuit above the northeastern coast, for which walking boots are recommended. The walk starts at the lovely bay of Kalami, which boasts a quiet pebble beach, a supermarket and a scatter of smart tavernas. The way climbs through olive groves and small villages to the austere, arid middle reaches of the island's highest mountain, Oros Pandokratoras (Mount Pandokratoras). Afterwards it plunges back to the glorious coast for an exceptionally pretty jaunt from cove to cove: walkers are spoilt for choice of swimming spots. The route is inadvisable in hot weather due to the ascent involved and the longish stretches where shade is a scarce commodity. Take plenty of water and food; the only café on the inland stretch is located at Porta, although once you're back on the seafront they are plentiful. Waymarking is fairly good except on the mountain, so follow the directions carefully.

The walk start **Kalami** is the location for the White House, the unmistakable cube building at the southern end of the beach, once the residence of members of the Durrell family.

Leave the southernmost end of **Kalami** by passing in front of the **White House**, then take the road uphill. As it bends right, go left on a concrete lane down through olive groves to where a path continues past vegetable gardens to the lovely secluded cove of **Gialiskari** beach. Turn immediately right up a white rock-based way, then soon left on a path alongside a wire fence. This leads over to pretty **Agni** beach. Walk past the inviting cafés and continue straight through the premises of friendly Nikolas Taverna and up past a large white stone house.

Pretty Agni beach

Not far along you leave the coastal path and fork right on a path with yellow paint markers, climbing steadily past private villas. You cross a road then proceed on an old stepped and paved way through well-graded terraces of olives and cypress trees. Where houses are reached, keep straight on along an alleyway and up to the square of **Kentroma** (**40min**) for views all the way to Corfu Town.

Turn left along the main road then take the first right, at a jasmine-scented corner, up a small road (with a CT sign). Only minutes up, as the road curves right, you're pointed left through masses of wild mint on old steps between dry stone walls. This ends at a road which is followed uphill past villas with swimming pools. A clearly marked path breaks off left for a steep climb and a short clamber before veering right on a more level path past stone walls. After fenced olive groves the road is joined once more. Branch left past a farmhouse where the antenna-studded top of Oros Pandokratoras is visible. Soon you turn left again on a rough stony track, but don't miss the faint path almost immediately right.

A bit overgrown in places, it leads through terraces and emerges on arid karst terrain. ▶

A road is joined up to a well-appointed **panoramic bench** near houses. Not far along a ridge is gained and a T-junction – go left for the peaceful mountain village of **Porta** (340m, **40min**). Pass the café and stick with the road uphill to the old school. Close by is a prominent church and war memorial, where wayfarers can rest and enjoy the well-shaded benches.

Just after the buildings go right on a path (yellow and blue waymarks) heading mostly N into woodland, rather overgrown in places. Cross a bridge, then it's up to cross a lane. Follow the blue n.9 markings scrupulously for the remaining distance to **Santa** (370m). Bear left through the tiny paved square and take the alleys threading their way between the houses. Keep left at the tarmac, up steps and left again at the road past new villas. Not far along you need the road forking uphill to **Mengoulas** (470m, **1hr**). ▶

This is home to birds of prey, and affords vast views across the water to the mainland.

The village's elegant stone houses are abandoned for the most part, and the village is populated by flocks of noisy jackdaws and laden fig trees.

Elegant stone houses at Mengoulas

At the circular village square, branch sharp left in front of houses and keep your eyes peeled for the way-marks leading up steps to the last buildings. Then, with superb views back over the Albanian coastline, a path makes its way past a low shepherd's hut and over the arid mountainside that doubles as pasture for sheep. This concludes at a stony lane (at 500m) which you follow to the left (S) for a magnificently panoramic stroll in the company of giant Jerusalem sage plants.

After a water **cistern** the summit of Pandokratoras towering over karst terrain comes into view as you reach a fork. Here you leave the CT and go left towards farm buildings, soon also parting ways with the blue-marked n.9 (which goes sharp left again). You continue straight ahead, due S. The level way passes over small quarries and becomes a rough stony lane. After a shed is passed Corfu Town comes into view at a wide stony **saddle** and fork where a pipe runs across the way. Go left here (SE at first) and stay with the lane following it around to veer right to a concrete-stone **cistern**. Here keep left (SE) in constant descent towards the welcome shade of cypress trees. Not long afterwards, at a derelict house atop a stone wall, yellow markers point you right to scramble down onto an old path through olive groves. Join a quiet road to the peaceful houses of **Katavolos** positioned dizzily over the coast. Leave the road at the parking area and walk left through to a spreading ilex tree shading stone slab seats – a perfect resting spot. Here it's right back to the road, which you leave at the next bend for a concreted lane (with CT waymarks) down past a new house. Then branch left on an unmarked path down old olive terraces alongside villas. Yellow paint marks reappear and point you left at the first junction for constant descent. This emerges on tarmac near houses and it's not far down to the main road (bus stop nearby).

Go left to the corner and take the concrete-based lane but don't miss the path that branches off it left for a winding descent through olive groves. A lane covers the last leg down to **Kaminaki** (**1hr 40min**), the glorious sea and a lovely waterfront lined with tavernas. Go L (NNE)

Approaching Gialiskari beach

to the end of the beach for a clear path along the rocky coast in the company of huge agave plants and secluded villas. It's not far to popular **Nissaki bay**, with its big hotel. Continue past the swimming pool to the bar then go left up steps and along the front of the hotel building to where the lovely path resumes, as does peace and quiet. Shaded by olive trees, it soon climbs steeply albeit briefly on steps to circle private property. ▶ Further along you pass the turnoff taken in the outward stage, and soon reach **Agni** beach and Nikolas Taverna. Now it's a matter of retracing your steps via **Gialiskari** beach back to **Kalami** (**1hr**).

The glittering turquoise sea is seen through the trees.

WALK 3
The Old Perithia trail

Start	Old Perithia
Finish	Almiros beach
Distance	9km
Ascent	150m
Descent	550m
Grade	2
Walking time	2hr 30min
Refreshments	Nothing until Almiros beach
Access	Old Perithia is located 8km inland from the main coast road: the turnoff (and closest bus stop) is at Perithia but you can always reach Old Perithia by taxi (tel 26630 32400 www.alfataxicorfu.net). At the end of the walk there are buses to Kassiopi or Aharavi in summer; otherwise Aharavi, 3km away, has the closest year-round service (walking along the beach to Aharavi takes about 40min)

This marvellous route starts out from the atmospheric semi-abandoned village of Old Perithia (Paleá Períthia) on the northwestern flanks of Oros Pandokratoras, and follows what was until around 50 years ago the settlement's sole access route, before the road was put through. It leaves the village to plunge through woodland and touch on a string of quiet rural hamlets on its way to the long sandy beach of Almiros on Corfu's north coast. Waymarking is not especially frequent. The walk coincides with a section of the last stage of the Corfu Trail.

The ancient village of **Old Perithia** – well worth a leisurely explore – is now a heritage site. Records attest to its existence at least as far back as the 1300s: some claim it was settled in 700bc. Long used as a refuge from pirate attacks, it was once home to 1200 souls who built 130 stone houses and eight churches. The inhabitants all left in the

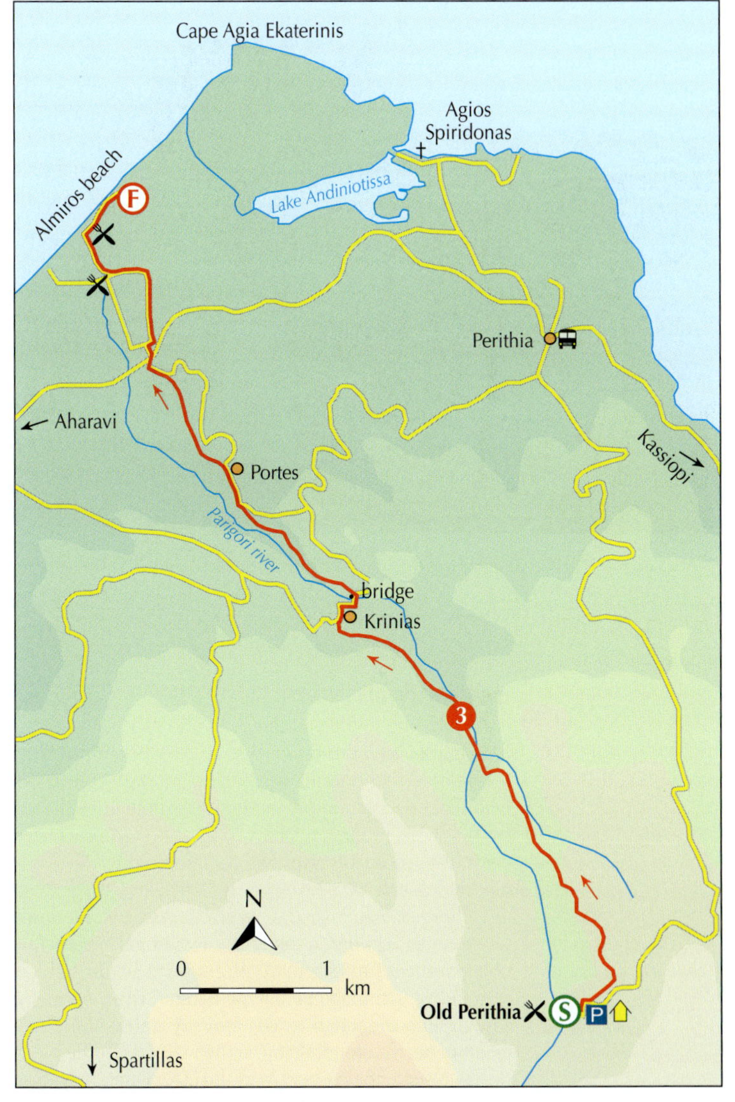

Cape Agia Ekaterinis
Agios Spiridonas
Almiros beach
F
Lake Andiniotissa
Perithia
Aharavi
Kassiopi
Portes
Parigori river
bridge
Krinias
3
N
0   1
km
Old Perithia
S
P
Spartillas

Al fresco taverna at Old Perithia

1960s, but the village is now gradually coming back to a rather different sort of 'life' with cafés, restaurants and even accommodation.

From **Old Perithia** the CT takes the lane below the car park, coasting initially N then bearing NNW. Where the lane comes to an end a path takes over, continuing in the same direction and descending through oak wood with ferns and accompanied by red/yellow arrows. Not far down all manner of flowering and scented shrubs encroach on an old way with stone edging descending the left side of a lovely gully-like valley, miles from anywhere. ◄ After several wide curves the gradient steepens as you enter shady dry woodland. Thereafter comes a beautiful stretch with relaxing bends, which conclude down at the bed of the **Parigori river**, normally strewn with bleached stones and dry unless there has recently been a cloudburst. The path climbs out the other side to resume the descent, and finally emerges on a lane

There are promising glimpses of the glittering sea ahead.

through olive groves. At a fork keep left over a rise to the handful of houses that go under the name of **Krinias** (140m, **1hr 25min**).

Turn right (NE) down the surfaced road as far as a bridge then go immediately left (NW) onto a lane. Where this concludes, a yellow marked path leads up to a concreted road. Follow this left to the nearby hamlet of **Portes** (100m, **20min**).

As the roads forks out of the hamlet, the CT goes left on a gravel lane (sign for public footpath) that is flanked by orchards. Soon becoming a path, it circles a fenced property and at the far corner you cross a lane and resume the path that heads slightly uphill to continue NNW through olive groves. Yellow waymarking reappears shortly and there are soon beautiful views to the lake and coast. After crossing another lane you enter shady oak wood with brambles and emerge on a road. Left here will quickly bring you out at the main coast road (**20min**). Cross over to the other side and turn immediately left (sign for Almiros beach) alongside rows of eucalypts. Then take the next right, which soon veers left towards the sea. Not far on, at Taverna Zephyros, fork right for the final run to the seafront. The rewards at the walk's conclusion, **Almiros beach (20min)**, are a glorious long white expanse of sand, the inviting George Taverna and views to the rugged mountains of Albania.

WALK 4

Around Cape Agia Ekaterinis

Start/Finish	Almiros beach
Distance	6km
Ascent/Descent	Negligible
Grade	1–2
Walking time	2hr
Refreshments	Tavernas at Almiros beach, Agios Spiridonas beach
Access	Almiros beach is reached by car on a signed turnoff 3km northeast of Aharavi. On foot from Aharavi (which is well served by year-round buses) walk through to the beach and turn right to follow the seafront all the sandy way to Almiros beach – allow 40min one-way

The glorious long white sandy expanse of Almiros beach looks over to the mountainous mainland of Albania and makes for a superb start to this easy loop, visiting the northernmost point of Corfu, beautiful Cape Agia Ekaterinis. The walk follows a rocky coastline dented with pretty coves and surrounded by masses of gorgeous Mediterranean flowers. Swimming spots abound, including lovely Almiros and Agios Spiridonas beaches, both of which also make pleasant lunch spots.

The central section traverses rocky terrain that is surprisingly jagged – sandals are unsuitable. Also, be aware there is very little shade en route.

From the George Taverna at **Almiros beach** head right (NE) along either the beach itself or the parallel lane, amid colourful clumps of wildflowers including crimson and yellow poppies. Where the beach ends, continue over a bridge. This crosses a channel connected with neighbouring Lake Andiniotissa, which remains out of sight here, so you now find yourself on an island.

Stay with the lane along the coast as far as a first pretty sandy beach, then continue straight ahead on a red soil path. This makes its way across surprisingly jagged

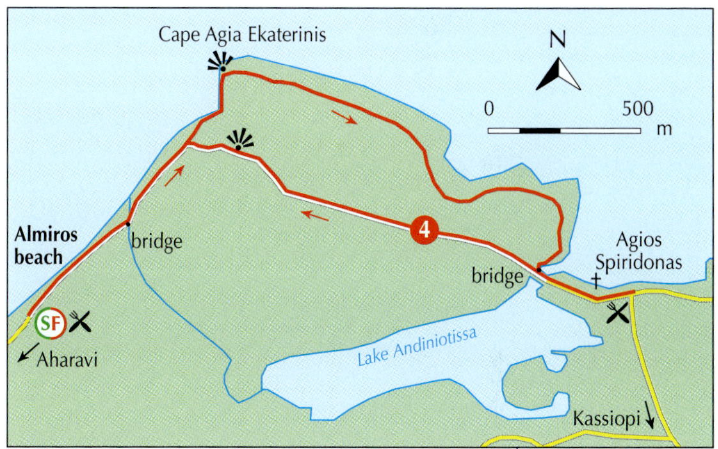

rocks, heading for the white beacon tower marking **Cape Agia Ekaterinis**, the northernmost extremity of Corfu. ▶

The clear path continues around the headland via a second beach. A little further on, as it reaches rocks, the way detours inland through tall grass to a lane. Follow this to the right and soon left across a **bridge** over a lake

This is a truly stunning spot.

At the first sandy beach

outlet near fish traps and nets. This brings you to the lovely beach of **Agios Spiridonas** (**1hr 10min**) backed by shady eucalypts, a chapel and an inviting taverna.

To return to Almiros beach, go back across the bridge and follow the lane NW between **Lake Andiniotissa** and the sea.

The attractive **inland lake** Andiniotissa is a haven for water birds. It was one of the Durrell family's favourite spots:

> *Up in the north of the island lay a large lake with the pleasant jingling name of Antiniotissa ... It was about a mile long, an elongated sheet of shallow water surrounded by a thick mane of cane and reed, and separated from the sea at one end by a wide, gently curving dune of fine white sand.*

This dune 'became a glacier of flowers' when the white lilies were in bloom.

There is an imperceptible climb to a rise near the ruins of a monastery, and views S to the Pandokratoras. Not far down you reach the first beach (see above) where the lane curves L (SW) for the bridge. Retrace your steps back to **Almiros beach** (**50min**).

WALK 5

The Panorama Trail above Aharavi

Start/Finish	Aharavi
Distance	12.5km
Ascent/Descent	530m/530m
Grade	2
Walking time	3hr 45min
Refreshments	Aharavi, Lafki (off-route)
Access	Aharavi is well served by buses

This is a long and tiring but rewarding walk with fairly good waymarking. It climbs from sea level using lanes and old paved pathways up to the 400-metre mark and the wonderful belvedere of Messovouno Hill, almost halfway up the northwest flanks of the limestone massif Pandokratoras. The rocky terrain means boots are recommended, as is a picnic lunch and drinking water.

Aharavi, where the walk starts, is the site of an ancient Greek settlement destroyed in 30BC by the Romans. The survivors took to the hills and a section of their escape route, known as the 'Secret Path', is followed during this walk. More historic interest comes with the Dandolo mansion towards the walk end.

Walk along the main street of **Aharavi** in the direction of Roda. Just before the museum and **Roman bath**, and near a blue 4 marker on a light pole, turn left on a lane past an old house with columns draped in grape-vines. ▶ Follow the guiding blue stripes and arrows to a stone farmhouse overgrown with brambles and branch left on a lane that enjoys coastal views. Not far along n.4 goes left through olive groves, first as a sunken path and then a series of winding lanes that brings you out at the well-tended houses of **Priftatika**.

Cross the road for a concreted lane, then leave this immediately for a path down through damp wood and across a bridged stream. The ensuing climb leads along

The way climbs gently S past small farms and vineyards, the coastal traffic buzz quickly left behind.

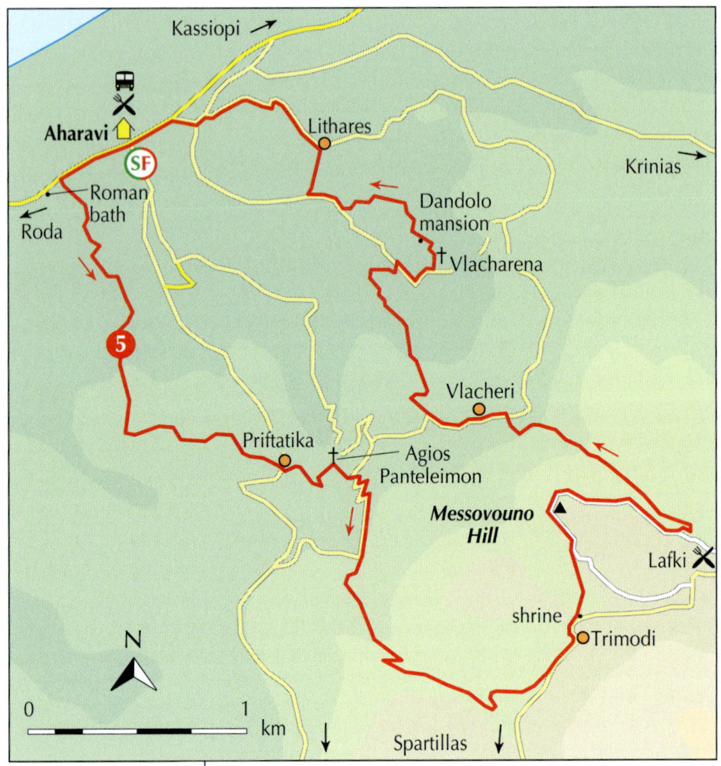

A short detour to the right touches on elegant manor houses, testifying to the erstwhile thriving olive business derived from the groves here.

fencing to the church of **Agios Panteleimon** (**50min**). The route proceeds up mossy steps between houses to emerge on a minor road. ◄

Follow the tarmac as it snakes uphill past ancient olive trees and white cliffs with views to the coast, now far away. As the road bends right, leave it for the narrow path breaking off left (blue n.7). If you reach a shrine you've gone a bit too far so turn back.

This is believed to be the start of the '**Secret Path**' followed by the refugees of Aharavi after the

Romans destroyed the settlement over 2000 years ago.

The partially paved way leads SE into a wooded valley dotted with wild orchids and cyclamens and dominated by rugged pale outcrops, an especially atmospheric place. Further up, as houses come into view, ignore a lane left and instead continue up to the road, which then leads left (NNE) to the tiny hamlet of **Trimodi**, (380m) in a world of its own.

At a nearby roadside **shrine** fork left on a lane which you quickly leave for a narrow steep path right, plunging into a valley thick with cypresses and ivy. The climb out the other side is through prickly vegetation on an

The shrine at Trimodi where the walk turns off the road

There are marvellous coastal views from Messovouno Hill

overgrown but well-marked path. This scrambles out onto a good lane which proceeds NNW to the marvellous open top of **Messovouno Hill** (416m, **1hr 10min**).

> This is the **highest point** on today's walk. The brilliant sweep of Corfu's northern coastline can be admired, along with Lake Andiniotissa and the view over the sea to the mountains of Albania.

Stick with the lane as it leads gently down E towards the village of **Lafki** and into a chestnut copse. Unless you opt for the village's cafés and tavernas, before reaching the houses turn left on a rough lane that winds in descent NW past an old well, walnut trees and woodland, overgrown in spots. ◄ As the lane ends (evidently the bulldozer got stuck here) the original narrow path takes over, dropping right down the wild damp valley, bright with cyclamens.

This is known locally as the 'Nun's Path'.

Further down woodland is replaced by olive trees: go left on a quiet surfaced road past the houses of **Vlacheri**,

The Dandolo mansion still stands

then right in constant descent past more scattered buildings. After passing between two villas with swimming pools you come to a bend where n.4 breaks off right as a lane. You soon need to ignore a branch left and continue downhill to a road – go right here in ascent in the direction of the mountain for about **5min**. Blue waymarks on a prominent cypress tree point you left onto a lane and the chapel of **Vlacharena**. Close at hand left, and partially concealed by trees stands the ruined **Dandolo mansion** (**1hr**).

> The overgrown but still impressive **Dandolo mansion** was once the stronghold of a prominent noble Venetian family. The three-storey fortress-like building even had a drawbridge. The elderly Doge Enrico Dandolo had been instrumental in the Fourth Crusade of 1202, which he craftily sidetracked to accelerate the end of Byzantium (Constantinople).

A path leads past the building and down to a lane, right. Be sure to follow the arrows and waymarks through the overgrown wood, across a stream bed, through to a chain then left at a concreted lane through olive groves. This leads out to tarmac where you go right. Immediately after two small buildings it's right again for a surprisingly steep uphill stretch past a fenced property to the houses of Lithares. Then it's all downhill, in the direction of the glittering, inviting sea. Keep left around a school and left again at a taverna, bringing you out at the main road near the Pumphouse restaurant, only a short way from the walk start in **Aharavi** (**45min**).

CORFU'S NORTHWEST

Rapidly eroding islands off Cape Drastis (Walk 6)

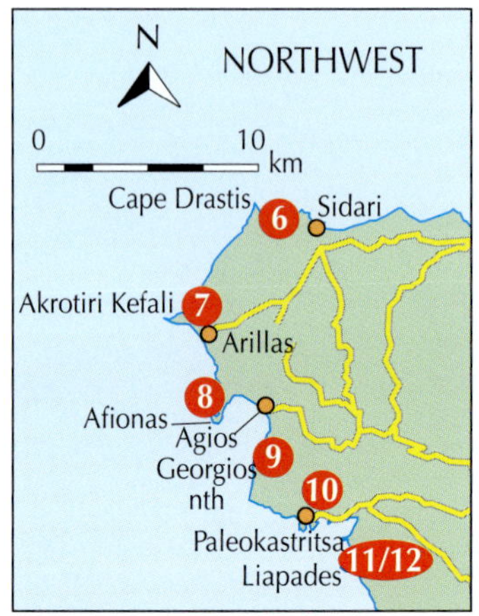

Some of the quietest beauty spots on Corfu are to be found in this corner of the island. Sightseers on coach trips flock to Sidari for the so-called 'Canal d'Amour', an eye-catching if rather over-rated attraction of natural channels at the foot of sandstone rock faces fast being eroded by the waves and currents. Of much greater dramatic impact is Cape Drastis, a short distance away. Walk 6 visits these precipitous white stratified cliffs on a spectacular photogenic headland. Sidari itself is a smallish if rather brash resort with a 'high street' lined with shoulder-to-shoulder trinket shops, cafés and bars that stay open into the wee hours. That said, it is not an unpleasant place to stay, as it offers plenty of accommodation and facilities, and is also served by bus.

Moving around the northwestern headland, the hilly coastline facing the Ionian Sea is dotted with small-scale resorts and the occasional village. Agios Stefanos is snuggled into a sheltered bay under the headland of Akrotiri Kefali – the name curiously repetitive as it means 'cape cape'. Beyond this is pretty Arillas, which boasts a lovely albeit narrow sand beach that faces the island of Kravia. Both Agios Stefanos and Arillas have hotels, shops and bus services, and are linked by Walk 7.

The next place worthy of note is the vast and beautiful bay of Agios Georgios north. It is sheltered by the stunning curve of the Porto Timoni headland where the belvedere village of Afionas stands – the two feature on must-do Walk 8. Both the beachfront and Afionas are lovely places to stay with a range of accommodation and seafront eateries. As transport goes, the rare bus comes as far as the beach. Walk 9 explores the beautiful southern opposite end of Agios Georgios bay, and the Corfu Trail also comes through here.

Paleokastritsa is simply gorgeous, a divine deep inlet of perfect blue dotted with tiny coves and enclosed by towering pale cliffs smothered in shrubs and greenery. According to legend one of the rocky islands floating off the coast saw the shipwreck of Ulysses. The fact that the hero had been given a ship so infuriated king of the sea Neptune that he conjured up a terrible storm. Nowadays a decent choice of hotels, restaurants and shops are clustered around the bays

and along the single access road; bus connections are good. A landmark monastery occupies a promontory along the main bay, while high above is the belvedere village of Lakones, not far from the marvellous fortress Angelokastro visited in Walk 10. Paleokastritsa aptly means 'place of the old castle'.

Back down on the waterfront at the innermost end of the inlet is the beach below the lovely village of Liapades, accessed by the occasional bus. Accommodation, shops and restaurants can be found on the road down to the beach and there are also plenty of cafés and tavernas in the pretty village square. Liapades is the start for Walks 11 and 12, leading to tiny photogenic coves that are reached on foot through well-tended olive groves – or by boat for the lazy.

WALK 6
Cape Drastis

Start/Finish	Mimosa Hotel, Sidari
Distance	10km
Ascent/Descent	200m/200m
Grade	1–2
Walking time	2hr 45min
Refreshments	Sidari, Melitsa
Access	The Mimosa Hotel, on the western edge of the resort, is close to the bus stop and taxi rank

Cape Drastis, with its spectacular wind-sculpted white cliffs towering a hundred or so metres above the brilliant turquoise Ionian, is one of Corfu's must-sees, and is easily accessed on foot, thanks to this superb and straightforward walk. The headland can also be approached by car via Peroulades, or by boat from Sidari.

Be aware that while Cape Drastis overlooks a stunning stretch of coast, the only spot for a swim en route is the cramped bay on the eastern side of the cape where access to the water entails a clamber. Save your swimming for Apotripiti beach on the way back to town. Trainers with a good grip are recommended for this partial loop walk, sandals definitely not as there are steep sections, and these can be slippery after rain. Waymarking, in the shape of blue markers and n.6, is pretty frequent. Take drinking water and a picnic.

By all means fork right here for the 10min signed detour to visit the Canal d'Amour.

From the Mimosa Hotel at **Sidari** walk W along the road parallel to the sea, in the direction of Peroulades. After the beachfront tennis courts turn right at the Three Little Pigs restaurant and continue over a bridge to a T-junction. ◀

Go left (W) past more shops and bars – and the fork for **Apotripiti Beach** – into a more rural landscape. About 1km from the T-junction, soon after the Selini Tourist Agency of **Melitsa**, take the path off right (**30min**), opposite a pole bearing blue marking n.6. If you reach

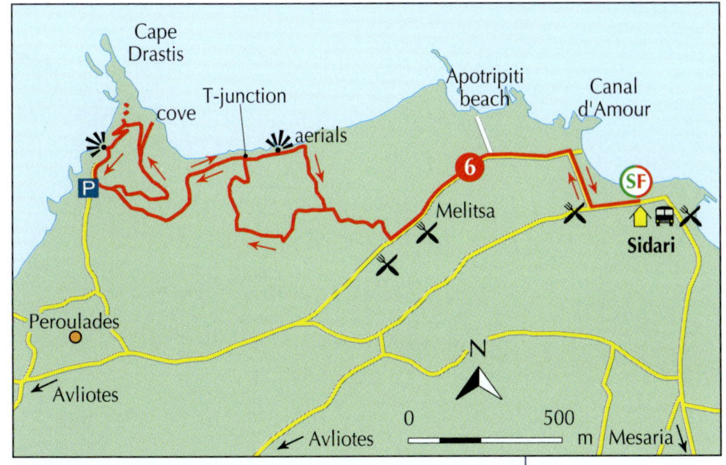

Alexis Restaurant you've gone too far. The clear way runs between wire fences to a lane and house where you branch left for a shady peaceful stretch mostly W in imperceptible ascent. As the gradient steepens the lane forks – go right through bracken across a dip before a climb to a rise thick with scented broom. Here at a **T-junction** a good hundred metres up, you get your first breathtaking view over the sea to the Diapontian islands and to the white cliffs including the dramatic Cape Drastis promontory that characterise this beautiful stretch of coast.

Turn left (WSW) along the scenic lane through masses of myrtle then olive groves as it bears briefly inland. After passing two sheds keep your eyes peeled for blue marking indicating a sharp fork right downhill in wide curves on a rough track. Further down this merges into a clay-based lane that quickly leads to a tiny **cove** with umbrellas and sun beds. There is no beach as such here, although swimming is possible. There is boat access too.

Return the way you came but stick with the main wide lane climbing N.

The tiny cove below Cape Drastis

Up at a saddle is a fork right for a private area for viewing Cape Drastis: a hefty fee is charged for access to an awesome lookout on the crumbling point. However by all means skip this and stick with the main lane curving SW to a free-of-charge fenced **belvedere** (**1hr**) with views over the dramatic cliffs and wonderful **Cape Drastis** headland.

Lord Byron apparently compared **Cape Drastis** to the white cliffs of Dover. Dizzy lookouts give marvellous views of lozenge islets progressively eroding due to the clay-sand-lime composition of the terrain and dissolving into the milky sea. This is said to be Corfu's closest point to Italy.

Further uphill is tarmac and a car park where n.6 turns left (SE) to resume the lane along the main ridge. Continue on this marvellously scenic route all the way back to the **T-junction** where you got your first wonderful views, but carry on E along the cliff top. This is an

especially lovely stretch overlooking the Ionian Sea. At a clutch of **aerials** in an olive grove is the last dizzy lookout – keep your distance from the edge as it's a hundred metre drop! Blue markers lead straight ahead, soon curving right (S) down a rough lane. At the bottom go left and back to the house encountered earlier on. Here it's right on the path put to the road at **Melitsa** for the return to **Sidari** (**1hr 15min**).

The Cape Drastis headland and its marvellous colours

WALK 7

Agios Stefanos to Arillas

Start/Finish	Margaritas supermarket, Agios Stefanos
Distance	5km
Ascent/Descent	150m/150m
Grade	1–2
Walking time	1hr 45min (1hr one-way)
Refreshments	Agios Stefanos, clifftop cafés, Arillas
Access	From Barros restaurant at the main turn-off for Agios Stefanos, head seawards (W); Margaritas supermarket stands at the next junction

This pleasant route links two attractive low-key seaside resorts via a clifftop lane on Akrotiri Kefali, a cape that offers wonderful views as well as a couple of cafés where you can make the most of them. Walking is easy on lanes and paths. The only potential tricky stretch could be the final descent to Arillas beach, which can get quite muddy, and hence slippery, after rain. Trainers rather than sandals are more suitable as footwear.

From the Margaritas supermarket at **Agios Stefanos** fork left (W) past Perditas Glass Art. This quickly brings you close to the beachfront and the Taverna O Manthos. Soon the road climbs gently to a grassy corner with a sweeping outlook over the lovely bay where Agios Stefanos nestles. But don't get too distracted by the views as you need to fork left just before the **FantaSea restaurant**. This steep road leads to a **Y-junction** and a squarish concrete pole where you keep right (W). You soon find yourself on a stony lane leading through scented bushes away from the houses, looking over to islands. Further up on the actual ridge and cliff top you veer left (E) at an isolated house not far from **Akrotiri Kefali**. ◄ A shrine is passed before a brief detour left to a photogenic white **chapel** amidst broom and cistus shrubs. Back on the main track a little further along is Arianna's Café with brilliant two-way

This is a lovely stretch looking down over Arillas bay and its sandy beach and out to Kravia island.

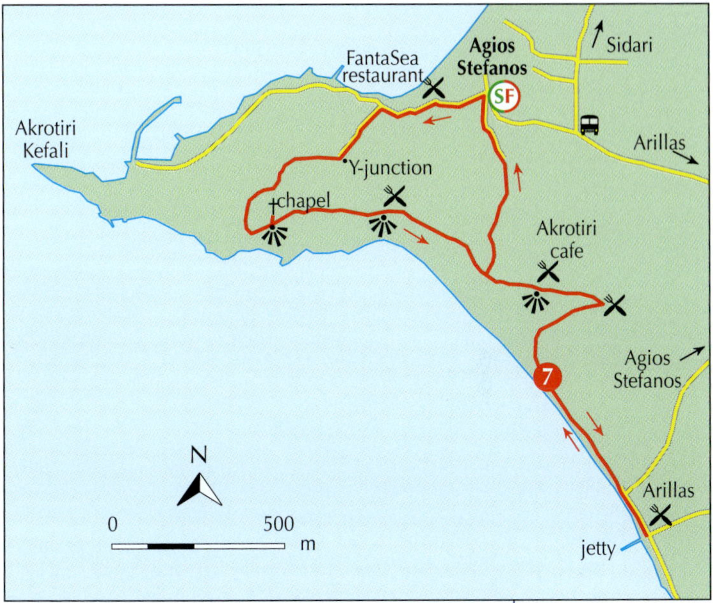

views. A clay-base lane continues uphill past houses to a fork (here the return route heads back left to Agios Stefanos) where you keep straight ahead for the elegant **Akrotiri Café**.

The white chapel near Akrotiri Kefali cape

The jetty at Arillas beach and Kravia island

Now the way begins to descend, reaching a junction and another panoramic snack bar. Here branch right down a stony track which can be muddy and slippery in places, not to mention heavily eroded. Once you've reached the inviting sea, either walk along the lovely sandy beach or stick with the parallel path through rushes. It's not far to the main beach and jetty of **Arillas** (**1hr**), along with a string of seafront eateries.

After a rewarding swim or lunch, return the same way uphill. Unless you prefer to retrace your steps the whole way back, just after the **Akrotiri Café** fork right down the lane, which will bring you out at Margaritas supermarket at **Agios Stefanos** once more (**45min**).

WALK 8
Porto Timoni

Start/Finish	Afionas church
Distance	3.5km
Ascent/Descent	150m/150m
Grade	2
Walking time	1hr 50min
Refreshments	Afionas
Access	No buses venture as far as Afionas, at the northern end of Agios Georgios bay. Either drive up and leave your vehicle at the car park just before the church, or walk from Arillas or Agios Georgios north beaches. From Arillas (50min) and the jetty opposite Restaurant Marina take the beachfront road S and stick with it as it turns inland. Not far along, opposite Feakes Apartments, branch right on the steep road with patchy tarmac. This leads through olive groves up to the ridge where you join the main road. Turn right past the Agios Georgios north junction, and on to Afionas. From Agios Georgios north (50min), follow the beachfront or the parallel road as far as Golden Moon Restaurant. Here turn right inland for the narrow road climbing to the ridge. Go left for the remaining 10min up to Afionas

Arguably the most beautiful spot on the whole of Corfu, Porto Timoni has twin coves that are accessible only on foot – or by boat or pedalo for the lazy. The local people will tell you that pirate ships used to take refuge here between raids on the coastal settlements. This wonderful spot is worthy of a drawn-out visit so by all means make a day of it. Wear shoes with a good grip as the path down is steep and stony, and can be slippery. In addition to sun protection, water and a picnic, don't forget swimming costume, mask and snorkel to enjoy the transparent water and multitudinous sea life.

After the inviting beaches, the walk extends to an atmospheric cave-cum-chapel devoted to Saint Stilianos. Afionas, where the walk begins and ends, is also a lovely spot. A handful of friendly panoramic tavernas beckon to weary walkers, while an excellent bakery produces delicious picnic food.

The church and war memorial at Afionas

Right from the start you enjoy superb views over the sweep of Agios Georgios bay.

Immediately after the church and adjacent war memorial at **Afionas** take the narrow concrete lane left, flanking a charming craft shop. ◄ It's not far along to where you keep left for a rough path through cypress trees below the panoramic terrace of the Taverna Dionysos. The clear way heads SW over rock surrounded by huge Mediterranean flowering bushes including cistus and oaks. Several rather high steps are encountered, so take care. Further down don't miss the short detour right to a belvedere for a bird's-eye view over the inviting bay and headland. Only a short distance away now, it's pure delight to reach **Porto Timoni** and the twin beaches (**30min**).

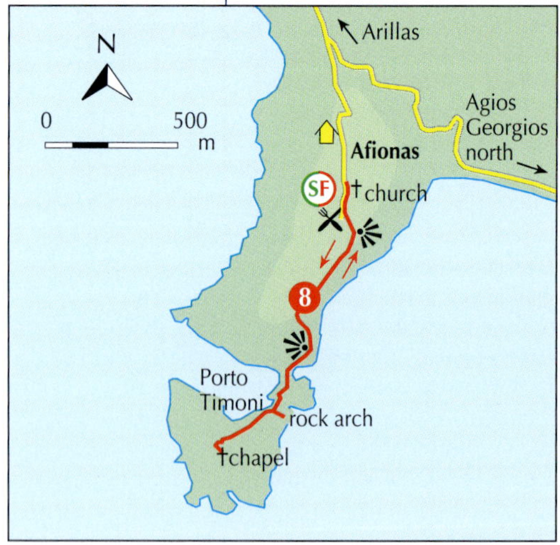

The clear path continues S at first in gentle ascent above the larger bay. Just around the corner detour left on a fainter path up to admire the awesome

The path from the beach at Porto Timoni to the cave

edge of a dramatic natural **rock arch**. Back on the main route continue SW coasting high above the lovely bay through thyme, cistus and strawberry trees, the vegetation encroaches on the path in places. Climbing, the way veers left uphill to the white cross marking the tiny cave-cum-**chapel** dedicated to Saint Stilianos (**20min**), crammed with ex-voto images.

> **Saint Stilianos** was a hermit and holy man from Turkey renowned for his warm smile. He is revered throughout Orthodox countries as patron saint of born and unborn children, after a miraculous intercession when he cured a woman of infertility and resuscitated a baby. Icons depict him holding an infant in swaddling cloths.

Return to the beaches (**20min**) for a swim and snorkel, before retracing your steps back up to **Afionas** (**40min**).

WALK 9
Fisherman's Cabin and the kalderimi

Start/Finish	Ostrako Tavern, Agios Georgios north
Distance	8km
Ascent/Descent	250m/250m
Grade	2
Walking time	2hr 45min
Refreshments	Agios Georgios north, Akrogiali Taverna, Fisherman's Cabin
Access	The start point is located on the southern end of Agios Georgios north beach, at the junction with the road from Pagi. The initial stretch as far as the Akrogiali Taverna gets badly eroded by winter storms and can be muddy in spring, however it is bulldozed punctually at the start of every summer as a decent motorable track.
Note	The return loop on the CT route is subject to landslip so you may need to retrace your steps.

A very enjoyable loop route that begins with a stroll along the seafront past a fish restaurant through olive groves to a quirky family-run eatery in a lovely isolated spot – well-reputed al fresco Fisherman's Cabin (tel 69425 85550 open for late lunch through to dinner; phone ahead if you count on eating there).

From there by all means retrace your steps, however the recommended continuation heads uphill to explore what's left of an old kalderimi (donkey track) climbing a spectacular eroding cliffside in wide curves with marvellous views. The return route, along a section of the Corfu Trail, cuts down the hillside through olive groves to rejoin the coastal lane. Drinking water and a picnic lunch are recommended. There are several small, secluded beaches en route, but none as nice as the main sandy expanse of Agios Georgios north.

From the Ostrako Tavern on the seafront at **Agios Georgios north** walk S along the minor road which becomes a dirt lane. After the **Akrogiali Taverna** stick with the bumpy lane through light woodland and olive groves parallel to the

sea. Ignore minor turn-offs, including the path fork where the return route joins up. It's a straightforward stroll with the occasional brief climb as far as the signs and menu boards for the short detour right, down to the laid-back **Fisherman's Cabin** (**45min**) overlooking the waterfront.

Press on for the steady winding climb away from the sea. At a junction, go left (E) on a lane partially paved with cracked concrete and in constant steepish ascent. After a stretch NW as this veers left (N), leave it for a faint rough path right onto the start of the old **kalderimi**

track. Unfortunately these lower reaches and the retaining embankment have collapsed in places so watch your step. But things improve and you soon find yourself on a wide lane edged with a low stone wall heading gently SW uphill in hairpin bends beneath cliffs thick with wildflowers and broom. The upper section concludes with a photogenic passage hewn through the cliffside with a spectacular view over the bay of Agios Georgios and the Diapontian islands beyond (**1hr**). Quite a spot!

Retrace your steps downhill to the lane at the end of the kalderimi. Here in common with the CT turn right then first left (N) through olive groves with glimpses of the blue sea through the trees. Following a series of tight curves the way narrows to a path down through reeds. Keep an eye out for a fork left on cobble stones in the company of brambles and olives. Down at the lower lane turn right past the **Akrogiali Taverna**, then follow the seafront back to **Agios Georgios north** again (**1hr**).

WALK 10

Paleokastritsa and Angelokastro loop

Start/Finish	Bus stop, Paleokastritsa
Distance	13km
Ascent/Descent	600m/600m
Grade	2
Walking time	4hr; visiting Angelokastro adds 45min
Refreshments	Paleokastritsa, Lakones, Krini, Angelokastro
Access	The bus stop can be found at the end of the main road into Paleokastritsa, near the Apollon Hotel

A spectacular fortress perched on a precipitous headland features on this brilliant must-do circuit walk – make sure you set out with a free memory card on your camera as the panoramas are breathtaking and never-ending. A fair few ups and downs are encountered, but short cuts can be made – see the sketch map and use the connecting roads. Lightweight walking boots rather than trainers are advisable in view of the stony paths: there are also unavoidable stretches of tarmac en route.

From the bus stop on the seafront at **Paleokastritsa** walk E along the main road to Kathy's supermarket and branch left uphill. Keep right where the road forks and up steeply past hotels. Soon after Ipsia Apartments you need the old donkey track off left signed for Lakones. The rough way climbs steadily through olive groves to meet a sheer limestone cliff face where the path bears right to follow the base. Further up it crosses a concrete lane and the path, narrower, proceeds to the quiet paved alleyways of the village of **Lakones** (240m, **45min**) where you emerge in the shady village square.

Short cut to Krini (30min)

Go left at Lakones and follow the busy road. After 2.5km you'll reach an **intersection** with souvenir stalls where you go left for Krini, as per the main route.

Prinilas
Vistonas
Makrades
Kastellani
intersection
10
stone column
Krini
stall
Lakones
monastery
Angelokastro
P
Corfu Town
N
0
500
m
Paleokastritsa
SF

The village square of Lakones

Turn right along the road for a couple of minutes to where a flight of steps heads up left between a butcher's shop and a batch of blue letter boxes. ▶

Climb straight up from the main road, ignoring turn-offs, to the last house where an old mule track forks right. The lovely cobbled way leads NE around Mount Arakli through flourishing bushes of cistus and aromatic herbs although you'll probably be distracted by the ever-improving views over Paleokastritsa. Up at a **stone column** (with a **church** to the right), turn left in descent on a lane used by sheep and goats. This brings you out on a minor road near a small **church**. Go left along the tarmac for half an hour in the company of olive trees and vineyards. The road descends a little and affords a dramatic view to the fortress of Angelokastro; soon afterwards you fork left – just before **Vistonas** (350m). A concrete lane leads down past a yellow **church** with a graveyard where a path continues straight ahead through an olive grove, cutting a wide bend in the road. Back on the tarmac it's

If you reach Anastasis Café you've gone a tad too far.

only steps away left to a sign for Taverna Colombos for the next short cut in the company of water pipes. The road is resumed for a final **5min** down to a fork – ignore the right branch (unless you need **Makrades** and its tavernas). Go left to an **intersection** busy with souvenir stalls and coach parking.

Now it's right on the narrow road for nearby **Krini** and its taverna. Walk through the tiny village square and continue S, soon in descent through olive groves and down to the picnic area, car park (**1hr 45min**) and friendly taverna at the base of the spectacular promontory housing Angelokastro.

From the ticket booth embark on the stiff but fascinating climb to enter the premises of **Angelokastro** by way of a stone gateway arch. From the top the views are simply breathtaking over the beautiful coastline. A tiny chapel marks the highest point (305m), alongside curious dug-out graves. Allow **45min** extra for the walk up and down and the fascinating visit.

The chapel and dug-out graves on the top of Angelokastro

The impressive fortress-cum-acropolis of **Angelokastro** dates back to the 1200s, the early Byzantine period. The name may derive from 'Angelo's castle', after a despot of Epirus who annexed the island to his region which now straddles Greece and Albania. It later fell into Venetian hands and became the governor's seat with a garrison. The castle occupies a strategic vantage point surveying the southern Adriatic and was a key lookout for shipping lanes, sending out warning signal fires to be relayed along the coast watchtowers to the fortresses at Corfu Town in case of danger. Multi-storeyed, it had its own underground vaulted water cistern. Angelokastro played a leading part in repulsing Ottoman attacks in sieges from the 1500s to the 1700s. A modest entrance fee is charged.

Afterwards head back up the hill on the road you took earlier. As you approach the village, immediately after a **stall** selling natural products fork right on a path with yellow/black CT marking. Follow this E through shady olive groves along low stone walls green with moss. Go left at a lane and where this peters out keep straight ahead to drop slightly to a dry stream bed where there is faint waymarking and a cairn. Fork left and out to the road. Follow this right downhill (SE) past a **monastery** and a string of superb belvederes and café-restaurants. On the outskirts of **Lakones**, at the premises of skilled olive wood artisan Alkis, branch right. A concrete ramp leads down to steps then a narrow path takes over, plunging in zigzags down olive terraces. At a concreted lane turn right through light woodland for the long winding way SW–E gently downhill. Scattered houses are passed then the road is surfaced down to Kathy's supermarket. Turn right back to **Paleokastritsa (1hr 30min)**.

WALK 11
Limni beach

Start/Finish	Bus stop, Liapades
Distance	5.5km
Ascent/Descent	150m/150m
Grade	1–2
Walking time	1hr 40min
Refreshments	Nothing en route
Access	The bus line to Liapades terminates at a T-junction on the western edge of the village; by car it is possible to drive down to the white painted letters on the lane, and park on the roadside

Limni (or Lemni) beach is a sand spit at the foot of a photogenic promontory with twin coves in the gorgeous bay of Paleokastritsa with its sheer limestone cliffs. It's an easy short walk from the village. By all means take a picnic and make a day of it. Instead of walking back afterwards, you can always jump on one of the boat taxis that ply the coast.

From the bus stop on the outskirts of **Liapades** take the road W towards **Liapades beach**. Pass a bakery then a church with a sizeable graveyard shaded by cypress

Inviting transparent water and the pebble beach at Limni

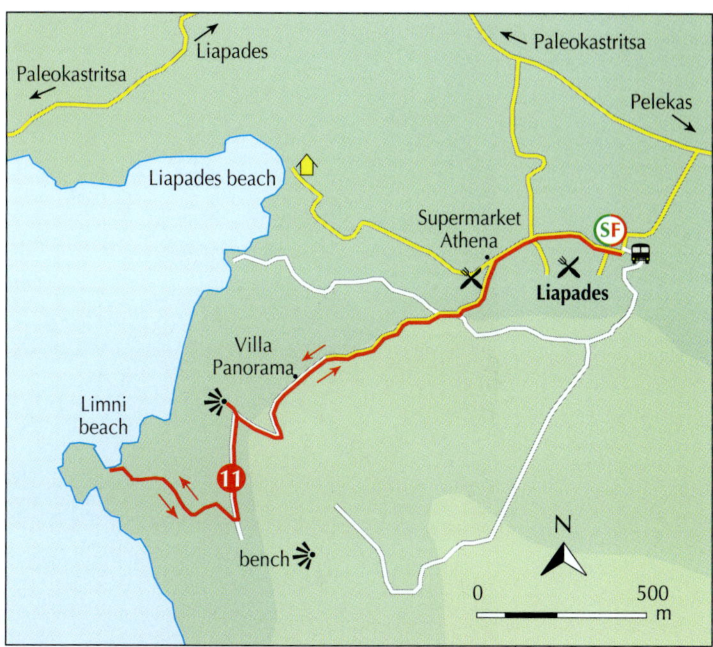

trees. At **Supermarket Athena** branch left uphill along-side the Vergina Taverna into olive groves. At the ensuing T-junction go right past a derelict brick building. Ignore the next fork right (yellow Corfu Trail markings) and con-tinue in ascent. Over a rise the narrow road levels out and you get the first glimpses of the marvellous sea and awesome cliffs on Paleokastritsa bay. The way becomes a concreted lane passing **Villa Panorama**. Stay with this as far as columns and a gate on the right side – detour for **5min** to the superb lookout over the attractive Limni promontory.

Resume the lane for the short distance downhill to where white painted letters point you sharp right (NW) down a shady lane. Not far along keep your eyes peeled for a wooden sign hanging in a tree and branch left onto a lovely path winding its way through a well-tended olive

The path through a well-tended olive grove

grove lined with low dry stone walls and a water pipe. Further on is a stretch of crazy paving followed by steps down to the beautiful twin pebble **beaches** and headland of **Limni** (**40min**).

After swimming, snorkelling, lazing around or picnicking, retrace your steps to **Liapades** (**50min**).

WALK 12

Linidoros beach

Start/Finish	Bus stop, Liapades
Distance	8.5km
Ascent/Descent	250m/250m
Grade	2
Walking time	2hr 50min
Refreshments	Nothing en route
Access	The bus line to Liapades terminates at a T-junction on the western edge of the village

The little-visited pebbly beach of Liniodoros nestles in a cove edged by low hills on the northern edge of the Akrotiri Iliadoros headland, worlds away from roads and resorts. Getting there entails a straightforward walk through woodland and well-tended olive groves, where the glittering blue sea is constantly glimpsed through the foliage. The return goes the same way, but the views over the spectacular Paleokastritsa bay are much better in this direction.

Make sure you go equipped with swimming costume, mask and snorkel, abundant drinking water and a picnic as this easily stretches out into a full day outing, although be aware there is no shade on the beach.

In common with Walk 11, leave the bus stop at **Liapades** on the road W for Liapades beach. Pass a bakery then a church with a sizeable graveyard shaded by cypress trees. At **Supermarket Athena** branch left uphill alongside the Vergina Taverna into olive groves. At the ensuing T-junction go right. Ignore the next fork right (yellow Corfu Trail markings) and continue in ascent. Over a rise the narrow road levels out and you get the first glimpses of the marvellous sea and awesome cliffs on Paleokastritsa bay. The way becomes a concreted lane passing **Villa Panorama** and reaches a big curve right. Soon afterwards take a stony way left uphill into woodland, mostly S. Ignore turn-offs and stick with the main

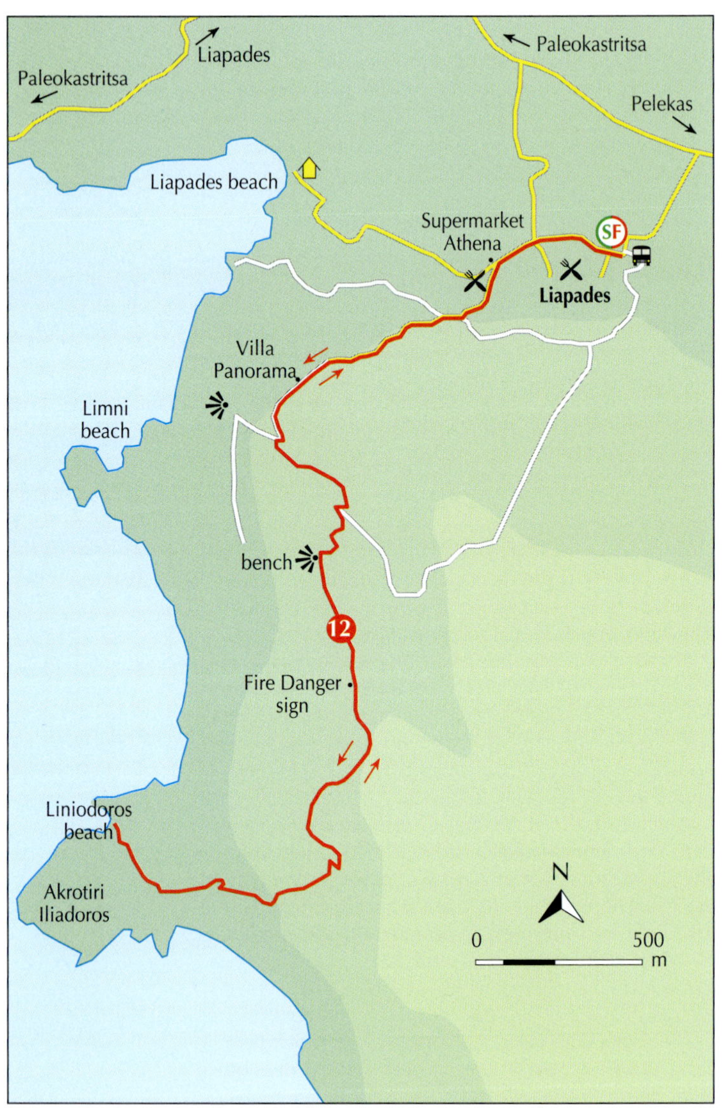

Paleokastritsa
Liapades
Paleokastritsa
Pelekas
Liapades beach
Supermarket Athena
SF
Liapades
Villa Panorama
Limni beach
bench
12
Fire Danger sign
Liniodoros beach
Akrotiri Iliadoros
N
0
500
m

lane which soon swings right through an olive grove to a tree trunk **bench**. Trees notwithstanding, this doubles as a decent lookout over the Paleokastritsa bay and north-west to the Angelokastro headland fortress.

The lane bears left (S) and ascends a little to a fork – keep straight on flanking a high stone wall. The way narrows to a path through more olive groves, coming to a junction with a **Fire Danger sign**. Don't be tempted by the right fork but continue straight ahead on a stony lane past terraces. You begin descending, gently at first, through Mediterranean shrub vegetation, then steeper and rougher until it's a veritable plunge. The happy conclusion is **Liniodoros beach** on the **Akrotiri Iliadoros** headland (**1hr 20min**).

At the inviting cove and white pebble beach of **Liniodoros** the turquoise sea beckons, while the adjacent low hillsides are covered with the scented

The Fire Danger sign and junction

83

The pebble cove of Liniodoros

curry plant and prostrate shrubs sculpted by the prevailing winds.

Retrace your steps back up the initially steep lane, and take care at the many junctions on the way back to **Liapades** (**1hr 30min**).

CORFU'S CENTRE

The panorama on the way down from Agios Georgios mountain (Walk 13)

An alluring range of landscapes is encountered across the island's centre, embracing both coastlines and mountainous interior. The magnificent eastern coast offers dramatic cliffs and summit lookouts in the vicinity of Pelekas, a charming hilltop town

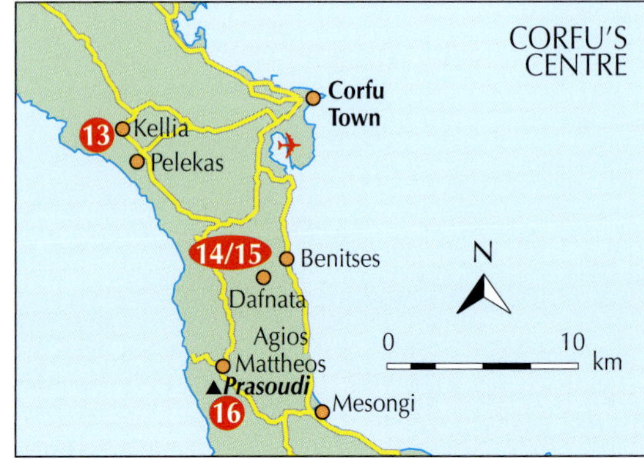

well-served with hotels, eateries and buses: the Corfu Trail makes an overnight stop here. It lays claim to the unusual 'Throne of the Emperor', a modest rock formation that doubles as a fantastic belvedere perched high above the settlement. It was named after Kaiser Wilhelm II, who much admired the views. A short distance northwest is the tiny village of Kellia (or Kelia) with bus services, shop, accommodation and a taverna. It is the start of Walk 13 which takes in Mirtiotissas, which is according to Lawrence Durrell

> perhaps the loveliest beach in the world...lion-gold sand, of the consistency of tapioca, lies smoothly against the white limestone cliff, thrown up in roundels by the force of the sea, which breaks upon a narrow sand-bank some sixty yards clear of the shore.

Further south, positioned exactly halfway across the island, is the lofty Agii Deka mountain, with its fine monastery. Needless to say it enjoys wide-ranging views. Agii Deka is the destination of Walk 14: the starting point, Makrata, is at the junction for the string of mountain-ridge villages known collectively as Stavros. The highest is peaceful Dafnata with a birds-eye outlook over Corfu Town.

Due east is the popular coastal resort of Benitses, start of Walk 15 to a historic aqueduct in the hills. Easy to reach by bus from Corfu Town, Benitses has plenty of hotels, restaurants and all manner of shops, although hardly a beach to speak of. The main coast road runs south to Mesongi before veering inland to a branch for the relaxed hillside village of Agios Mattheos. Surrounded by densely wooded reliefs surrounding the belvedere mountain of Prasoudi, this is where Walk 16 starts: it offers eateries, shops and the occasional bus.

WALK 13

Mirtiotissas and
Agios Georgios mountain

Start/Finish	Bus stop, Kellia turn-off
Distance	7km
Ascent/Descent	400m/400m
Grade	2
Walking time	2hr 45min
Refreshments	Kellia, Mirtiotissas beach
Access	Catch the Glifada-bound bus from Corfu Town and alight at the Kellia turn-off at Villa Natassa studios opposite a café; drivers can park near the church

A long but superb rewarding circuit that takes in Mirtiotissas beach, verging on paradisiacal in Lawrence Durrell's day, although now rather reduced in size as winter storms have carried much of the sand out. Nowadays it is known as the island's unofficial nudist beach. A peaceful monastery has occupied a lovely spot above the beach for centuries, surviving pirate raids along with the ravages of time. After the beach comes a stiff ascent to Agios Georgios ('St George'), a brilliantly panoramic mountain ridge, undeniably one of Corfu's top belvederes.

Boots or non-slip trainers are essential for the stony terrain, and you should carry plenty of drinking water. A swim is definitely an option but don't relax too much as a stiff 400m climb to the mountaintop awaits immediately afterwards! Naturally the walk is doable in the opposite direction, although it can be tricky finding the path turnoffs – be warned.

From the bus stop fork right (W) for the short distance to the attractive 13th century **church** of Agios Nikolaus at Kellia. Here go left on a signed path along the edge of a field and into an olive grove. After a rusting pick-up van the way widens to a lane and continues on to a narrow tarmac road. Follow this right over a rise then decidedly downhill, plunging past a **café-restaurant** on a lane. You quickly reach the beautiful rocky bay with **Mirtiotissas**

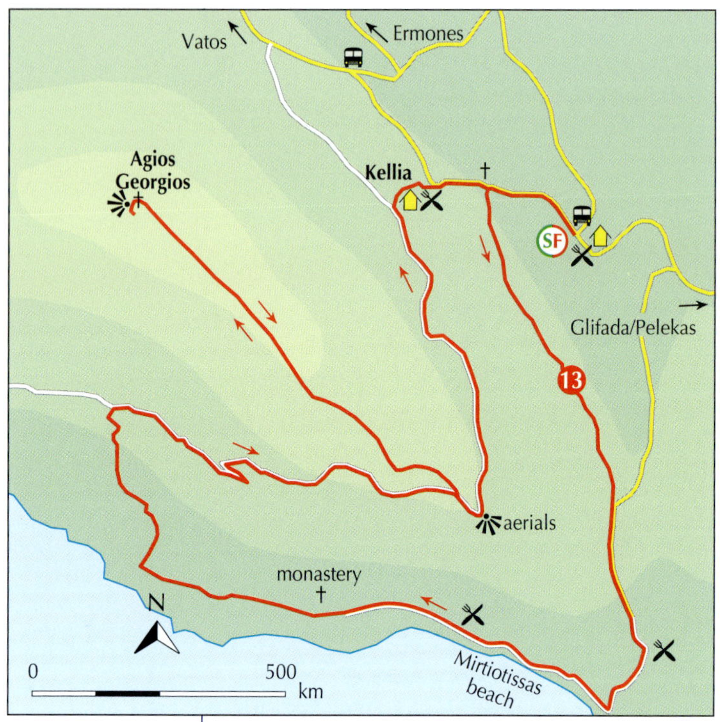

beach (**30min**), passing along the foot of awesome sheer cliffs where broom and even conifers hang on precariously. Then it's uphill past the Bellavista taverna to the imposing gates of the well-kept **monastery**. Without entering the premises branch left past a bench below the buildings on a path soon climbing through olive groves. It's steadily uphill past derelict farmhouses to a junction with a partially concreted lane. Go right (E) for a steep slog. ◄ The lane levels out as it cuts across the midriff of Agios Georgios mountain. Shortly before a patch of **aerials** (200m), you need the path left signed for 'St George'.

This well graded way climbs steadily NW through masses of flowering cistus bushes, the views improving

step by step. It's a route to be savoured. Further along the ridge stands a tiny white 12th century chapel, on **Agios Georgios** (403m, **1hr 15min**).

The tiny 12th-century chapel on Agios Georgios

> This is a **breathtaking spot**. Go for a wander along the ridge top and drink in the magnificent vision taking in virtually the whole of the island, from the Pandokratoras in the north, the Ropa valley close at hand inland, Corfu Town due east, then the Albanian-Greek mainland beyond and the lovely east coast dotted with bays and beaches.

Rested and inspired, return all the way down the path to the lane. Go left to the **aerials** (200m). Not far over the other side near a power pole ignore the rough path branching right in descent (CT) and stick with the partly surfaced lane gently descending N. Further down turn right on a signed old pathway through olive groves and houses, to reach the grocery shop and café Spiros Taverna. Out at the road branch right back to the church at **Kellia** and on to the bus stop (**45min**).

WALK 14
Agii Deka

Start/Finish	Makrata
Distance	7.5km
Ascent/Descent	300m/300m
Grade	2
Walking time	2hr 15min
Refreshments	Makrata
Access	On the Corfu Town–Strongili road, Makrata is at the signed junction for Stavros, a group of villages. It is best reached by car as buses are rare. Walk 15 also comes through here, and can be used to access the walk.

A medium altitude circuit walk with bags of variety in landscape and panorama that climbs to the Agii Deka, meaning 'ten saints', although the mountain is often referred to as Pantokrator, for its chapel and monastery – confusingly like the island's principal peak in the northeast. The highest point of Agii Deka is out of bounds due to the presence of a radar installation that resembles a giant golf ball, but the peaceful monastery premises nearby are always accessible.

The outward stage of this walk uses the Corfu Trail, following paths with steep sections, while the descent loops back on a straightforward broad lane that regales the walker with ongoing views over the east coast.

Leave the road at **Makrata** (250m) for a quiet concrete-based road leading due W and signposted for Pantokrator. After a shrine then a chapel, continue gently uphill past a field then branch left off the road at a brick wall. Heading mostly W again the way quickly narrows to a clear path over streams in damp woodland, then wanders past pencil-straight cypresses and through long-abandoned olive groves where stone terraces are thick with moss. Well marked, it continues past huge boulders of pebble conglomerate, the atmosphere reminiscent of a ghost village. A lane takes over, leading past scattered huts under

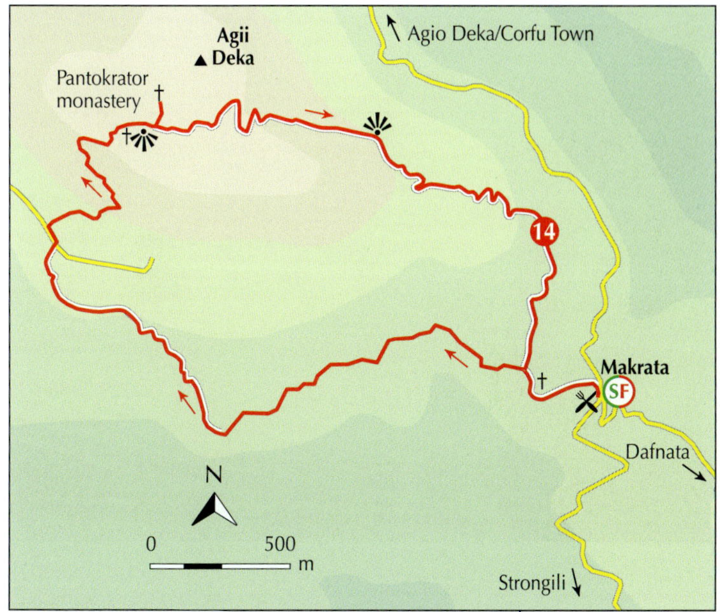

olive trees, climbing steadily WNW as views open up. At houses and a minor road go left then first right to pick up a narrow path.

After a short level stretch, brace yourself for a stiff climb winding mostly NW over olive terraces. A flatter section crosses ivy-smothered wood before a steeper section. This concludes at a whitewashed chapel in a marvellously panoramic clearing on the edge of the **Agii Deka** mountain with views over to both the east and west coasts of Corfu, as well as the giant radar golf ball closer at hand on the neighbouring mountain. Head down the lane then turn left for the **Pantokrator monastery** (530m, **1hr 30min**) with a peaceful garden shaded by spreading trees. ▶

Go back out of the monastery premises and ignoring the fork right for the whitewashed chapel, continue straight ahead (E) on the lane, uphill at first. Not far along

Don't miss the church with its wonderful painting of Pantokrator, Christ the Almighty.

it passes the fork for the radar installation, then starts gentle descent in the company of superb views over the scattered settlements of Stavros, as well as Corfu Town and the mountainous mainland beyond. Mediterranean oaks, strawberry trees and cyclamens line the way. There are a couple of minor dips and climbs, and side tracks to be ignored. After houses, the relaxing route concludes back at the road at **Makrata** (250m, **45min**).

WALK 15

Benitses to Dafnata

Start/Finish	Benitses
Distance	7km
Ascent/Descent	300m/300m
Grade	2
Walking time	2hr 30min
Refreshments	Makrata, Dafnata, Benitses
Access	The main bus stop at Benitses is located on the Corfu Town–Mesongi road near the marina.

This worthwhile loop route takes you away from the coastal crowds to a string of mountain villages via an old path flanking remnants of a historic aqueduct. It makes for an interesting walk, and there's even a short underground tunnel to be admired. Occasional waymarking guides you – in the shape of a red painted walker figure on the way up, and white/blue arrows on the way down. Be aware that both the ascent and descent paths can be slippery if wet. There's a stretch of tarmac on the middle section. Fit walkers can extend the route by combining it with Walk 14 for a total of 4hr 45min, although be aware this also will mean a cumulative height gain/loss of 600m.

From the bus stop at **Benitses** turn inland from the sea-front to cross the square, and follow a sign for 'Old Village'. Passing a supermarket and restaurants the narrow road curves left then almost immediately right, alongside a whitewashed wall, before dividing at a white house. Keep left and on past a Chinese restaurant and a minuscule yellow church, then continue through houses and down to cross a bridge.

At a **car park** and **five-way junction**, take the third from the left, near a stream. This crosses another bridge and heads up to railings near large black pipes, a sure sign you're on the right route for the aqueduct. Steps lead up to a **church** and a graveyard. A path soon takes

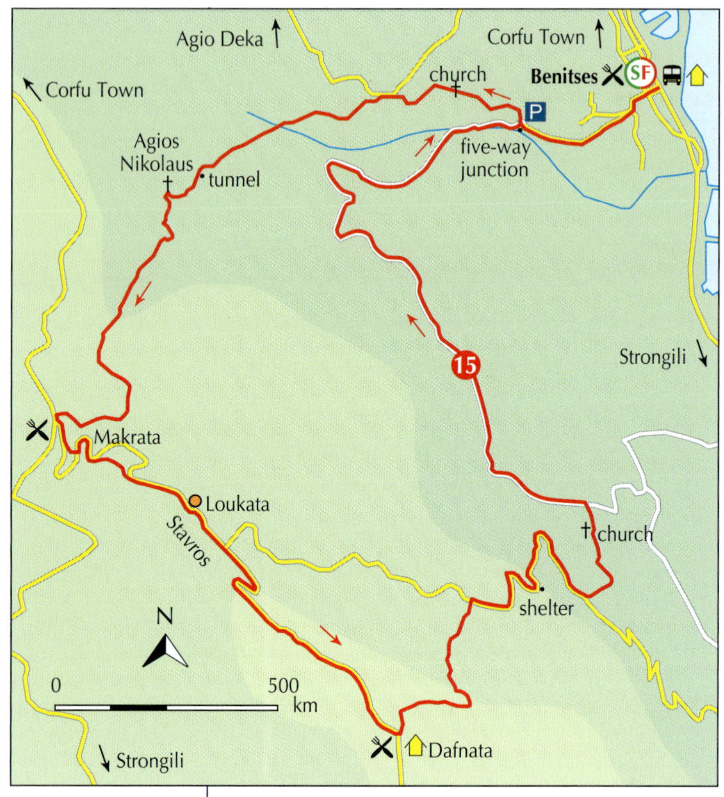

over, becoming a concrete lane uphill near a water treatment plant. As the lane curves right, leave it for the clear path straight ahead, through to a house and up steps to a minor road. Here at two shrines a sign for 'water springs' points you left past houses to a raised level walkway with railings, a lovely stretch. Heading into woodland bright with cyclamens, you climb gently to an old **tunnel** which once transported water for the aqueduct. Steps climb around it to the church of **Agios Nikolaus** with a sheltering porch and benches.

The aqueduct tunnel

Inaugurated in 1831, the **aqueduct** was the brain-child of the British High Commissioner Sir Frederick Adam, whose objective was to supply thirsty Corfu Town with fresh water channelled from the copious natural springs on the mountainsides above Benitses. It cost £19,386 and took 10 months to construct. However, it was neither the first nor the last attempt to settle the ongoing water shortages: the ancient Romans as well as the Venetians had masterminded earlier projects.

The aqueduct's remains are left behind for a steeper constant climb through olive groves and damp wood, often close to a stream. Just above a shed is a concreted lane where you go right to the nearby road at **Makrata** (250m, **1hr**). ▶

Unless you need the adjacent café, fork sharp left up the Stavros road. By all means short cut the first bend via the church. Not far up, to avoid some of the tarmac, fork right opposite the bus stop then next left along a narrowing alley between abandoned houses. Back on the road you pass an ancient bakery, its low roof held up with forked olive branches. After the houses of **Loukata** ignore the road turnoff for Benitses and push on for the

Opposite is the signed lane for the Pantokrator monastery on Agii Deka – see Walk 14.

belvedere of **Dafnata** (320m, **20min**) with a friendly taverna and a genuine UK phone box. ◄

Branch sharp left down a steep concrete lane which quickly becomes a rough track. Keep your eyes peeled for arrows pointing you left onto a path that winds its way mostly NNE down through abandoned olive groves thick with brambles and bracken. This plunges to a minor road in the company of cypress trees. Follow the tarmac down a couple of bends past a wooden **shelter** and a wide corner with a view over Benitses and to the promontory of Corfu Town. Not far on the path resumes left (arrow marker) into olive groves and through to a charming **church** with resident cats, and a giant cypress as well as a massive oak tree propped up by a pillar. ◄ Leave the premises under the arch of the belfry to a lane. Here arrows point you left (NW), to the base of a mountain flank and fallen boulders. Ignore a fork right and stick with the lane, bearing inland and gently uphill at times. Further along, a decisive swing right (E) marks the start of the descent, past houses with vegetable plots and a basketball court, to the five-way junction encountered earlier. Turn right across the bridge and back through **Benitses** to the seafront again (**1hr 10min**).

WALK 16

Agios Mattheos and Prasoudi

Start/Finish	Car park, Agios Mattheos
Distance	5.5km
Ascent/Descent	350m/350m
Grade	2
Walking time	2hr 15min
Refreshments	Agios Mattheos
Access	The car park is in the village centre

Agios Mattheos is a lively mountainside village with a main street of shoulder-to-shoulder shops, cafés and al fresco tables. This peaceful walk explores the neighbouring mountain of Prasoudi. Its perfect conical shape is instantly recognisable from the west coast where it is reflected in the still waters of Lake Korission. This fine walk does a stiff 350m uphill, but the reward comes in the shape of superb views from a veritable eyrie. After winding up past the tiny, well-kept pastel-stuccoed village houses tucked along narrow alleyways, an ancient way is taken up to the Pantokrator monastery and two belvederes, both gorgeous spots. The descent route takes a straightforward wide lane.

Boots or trainers are recommended footwear. Blue paint markers indicate the route to the monastery.

From the car park at **Agios Mattheos** (120m) turn right up the main street past the open-air cafés. Take the first street left (with a taverna on the corner) and follow the narrow ascending road lined with houses to a T-junction and a power pole plastered with posters. Branch right here along an alley that concludes at the lovely village **church** with a spreading shady tree.

Now you need the road sharp left (SW) for a steepish climb. It quickly narrows to a lane, bears right alongside a white house and heads into an olive grove, becoming rougher and stonier as it winds uphill. At a wide unsurfaced road go right to a faded wooden signpost at a bend.

An alley leads through to the main church

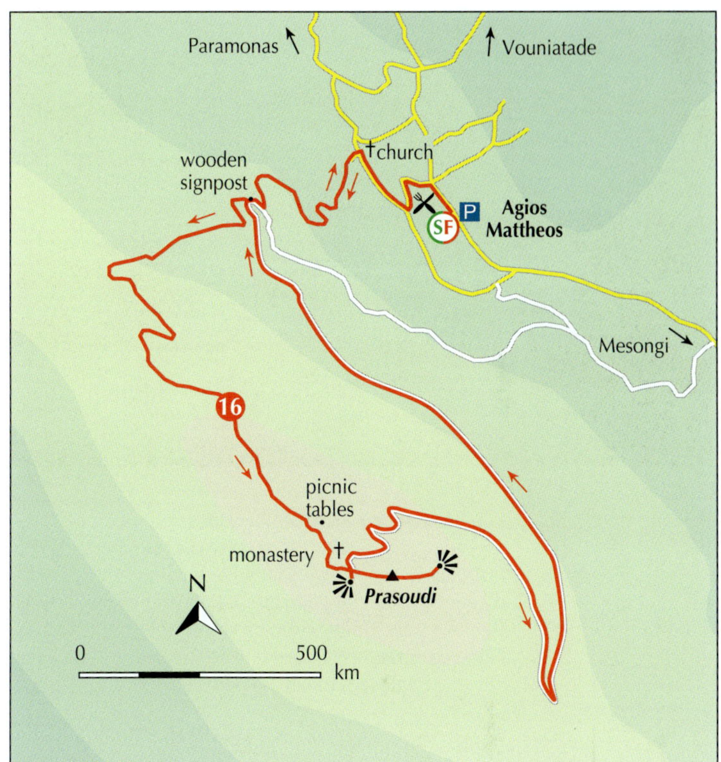

This marks the start of the delightful ancient pathway that, clear and well-graded, climbs past old terracing thick with moss into shady woodland of holm oak and shrubs. A long stretch SE finally concludes at a clearing with **picnic tables** at the Pantokrator **monastery** (**1hr**). Take the path leading right around the walled premises to the rear and the belvedere on **Prasoudi** (468m), marked by a metal pole and a bench. ▶

The path continues E past stone ruins to a path junction and a second **viewpoint** (**30min**) – this time over the Agios Mattheos village and both of the island's coasts.

This is a wonderful lookout over Lake Korission and the west coast.

The mountainside village of Agios Mattheos

Retrace your steps to the monastery perimeter wall and go right through to a lane. Follow this in descent E at first then swinging NW with wide-ranging views over the wooded hills and settlements. Back down at the wooden signpost, keep on the short distance for the fork (left) you came up earlier. This leads back down to the church and village of **Agios Mattheos** (**45min**).

The riverside at Potami (Walk 20)

Bearing a remarkable resemblance to the back leg and hoof of a horse, the southernmost part of Corfu stretches down into the Ionian Sea. While less dramatic than the mountainous north, it has some memorable natural beauty spots and has a lot to offer walkers. Top of the list comes Lake Korission, a protected nature area and the island's most extensive body of inland water – 24sq km. Home to herons and swans, the lake also provides refuge for exotic migratory species in spring and autumn. Its neighbour, Halikounas beach, is without a doubt the island's most beautiful expanse of sand – and is thankfully undeveloped, unless you count a handful of laid-back seafront cafés. A bridged channel and a low rocky headland are all that separate it from the adjoining stretch of golden sand that includes Issou (also confusingly known as Issos) and Agios Georgios south. Heaven! The lake and beaches are the highlights of Walks 17 and 18 beginning at Agios Georgios south, which is served by bus in summer and has plentiful accommodation and eateries.

Nestling in the hills a short distance to the northeast is the charming hillside village of Chlomos (or Hlomos), visited by Walk 19. The whole place is a viewpoint par excellence, looking up the east coast of the island and over to the mainland.

Lefkimmi is worth a visit. A spread-out grouping of villages, it forms Corfu's second largest town, its importance partly due to the ferry port on the far east coast. Notwithstanding, the atmosphere is utterly relaxed, and no more so than at Potami, site of the canal-like Himaros river (*potami* itself means 'river'). Strategic for transporting goods to the coast in Venetian times, it now has cafés and tavernas strung along its banks. The Corfu Trail stops over here and there are buses, accommodation and of course shops. Just off the point of Lefkimmi are extensive salt pans, all but abandoned nowadays but a fascinating stroll in Walk 20, taking in the wetlands and varied bird life.

Kavos (also spelt Cavos) is to be found in the far southeast, the bottom end of Corfu as it were. A sleepy place throughout the winter when it goes into hibernation, it mutates into a non-stop party venue over the midsummer months, not terribly inviting

for walkers. That said, in spring and the end of summer the attractive long sandy beach can be enjoyed in peace and quiet. As well as the launching pad for the long-distance Corfu Trail, it is a handy base for Walks 21 and 22, and offers abundant hotels, rooms, shops and buses from Corfu Town.

WALK 17
Lake Korission circuit

Start/Finish	Linia turn-off, Agios Georgios south
Distance	18km
Ascent/Descent	Negligible
Grade	1–2
Walking time	4hr 30min
Refreshments	Agios Georgios south, Issou, Linia, Lake Korission, Halikounas beach
Access	Begin from the far western end of the sprawling resort, at the Linia turn-off signposted for Corfu Town, near the seafront Bistrot restaurant; if you have a car by all means slot into the walk at Halikounas beach.

Placid Lake Korission is circled on this excellent route. The lovely lake-cum-lagoon is separated from the sea by a slender but well-consolidated sand bar colonised by a brilliant palette of colourful wildflowers. The lake was used for fish breeding during the Venetian era and a channel cut through to the sea. The outward stretch of the walk is a lengthy wander along lanes through olive groves and cultivated fields, not to mention thickets of colourful prickly pear. As waymarking is all but absent, it's essential to keep an eye out for landmarks and follow directions carefully so as not to miss the many turn-offs. More relaxing is the straightforward home leg along the lakeside, sand dunes and beachfront where stop after stop for a swim in the inviting sea will inevitably slow progress.

The walk is inadvisable on hot days as there is very little shade. Along with sun hat, suncream and swimming costume, take plenty of drinking water. Trainers are fine for this walk, and bare feet are just the thing on the concluding beach section. A shorter version can be followed in Walk 18.

From the Linia turn-off at **Agios Georgios south** stay on the road parallel to the seafront, past the Evergreen Café, restaurants and the tiny harbour to where the tarmac ends near a supermarket. Continue past the Aquis Sandy Beach resort and across a bridged stream on a sandy

Kato Spileo
Hlomatiana
Corfu Town
Agios Mattheos
Alonaki Bay
Villa Zaira fork
church
green buildings
Bioporos
quarry
four-way junction
church
Halikounas beach
footbridge
Lake Korission
Walk 18
Issou beach
Agios Georgios south
SF
Lefkimmi
Linia
P
17
N
km
1
0

The lane is lined with huge prickly pear plants

If you reach the nearby main road you've gone too far.

track through low juniper shrubs. This will bring you out at the café and lookout tower at **Issou beach** (**20min**). Go right here inland through a car park and onto a dirt road NNE flanked by palm trees, myrtle and wild mint bushes. Ignore the lane left for the lake (it peters out), and walk on past a café-restaurant, now on tarmac. As the road curves uphill right for nearby **Linia** and its café, branch left at an electricity pole onto a narrow road NW through olive groves. The odd house is passed and there are views down to the lake and dunes.

After an old hut on the left side take the lane forking left past a tiny **church**. ◄ This ensuing scenic stretch is in gentle descent to a Y-junction where you keep right through a rural landscape At a **four-way junction** take the first branch right to head N inland through an avenue of myrtle and soon cultivated fields. Ignore turn-offs until a T-junction near a small **quarry**.

Now it's sharp left (WSW) downhill with stretches of concrete. At the next T-junction at a house go right following a power line and poles. Only minutes along ignore the left branch and bear right in gentle ascent again through olive groves. ▶ At a track crossroads keep straight ahead under tall shady holm oaks, and soon to yet another T-junction. Here it's right gently uphill to a concreted lane at a fenced property. Branch left here (signed for Bioporos) and stick with this lane NW past eucalypts to green buildings.

Unless you hanker after refreshments or a relaxing lunch at **Bioporos** (in which case turn left), continue straight ahead past cypress trees then a blue house on a hill. A lovely scenic stretch soon goes downhill in the direction of the lake. Where the way goes left, leave it for a faint fork right, marked with red paint. Only minutes along near a gate to a property, keep right then in descent flanking a barbed wire fence. Red waymarks lead you across a rough stretch to join up with a better lane. Over a rise a good view of Prasoudi mountain looming ahead north is enjoyed. Not far on is a tiny white **church** in a field. Further on is a pink house preceding a lane **fork** with a sign for Villa Zaira. Turn left here past a white house with a satellite dish and other villas set in olive groves. The lane veers right through vineyards, finally dropping to the lakeshore. Proceed right, out to a road with a taverna on the corner. A short stroll to the left is glorious **Halikounas beach** (**2hr 20min**).

Here either take the lane left (SE) or walk along the sand via two well-organised beachfront cafés that provide shade, food and drink with a glorious outlook. The lane runs along a sand bar between Lake Korission and low dunes colonised by sprawling juniper shrubs, broom, tamarisks and massive clumps of exquisite lily-like white sea daffodils that bloom for months. Further along you come to a red fisherman's hut populated by ravenous cats. Cross the **footbridge** (**35min**) over the Venetian-era channel and go left past heaps of dried seaweed. The lane immediately veers right along the lovely lake edge, in and out of tree and shrub vegetation that provide some shade. Stick with the sandy lane as it continues mostly SE to cross the dunes. You end up down on glorious sand and saunter along to **Issou beach**, and on to finish in **Agios Georgios south** (**1hr 15min**).

Over a rise are excellent views to the lake as well as the bridged channel to Lake Korission.

WALK 18

Short Lake Korission route

Start/Finish	Linia turn-off, Agios Georgios south
Distance	11km
Ascent/Descent	Negligible
Grade	1
Walking time	3hr (one-way 1hr 30min)
Refreshments	Agios Georgios south, Issou, Halikounas beach
Access	Begin from the far western end of Agios Georgios south, at the Linia turn-off signposted for Corfu Town, near the seafront Bistrot restaurant; if you have a car by all means begin the walk at Halikounas beach and follow the directions in reverse

This walk takes you along a long sandy beach before crossing flower-smothered dunes to the shores of Lake Korission, concluding at gorgeous Halikounas beach. Do wander off-route through the sand dunes bright with spring blooms and hardened sand formations reminiscent of Arizona in miniature. It is easy to become disoriented but you can't go wrong by heading towards the sea.

Unless you set out very early, this walk is inadvisable on hot days as there is no shade. Carry drinking water as well as a sun hat, suncream – and a swimming costume. Sandals are fine for the lanes, and naturally bare feet along the beachfront. A longer version is followed in Walk 17.

From the **Linia** turn-off at **Agios Georgios south** stay on the road parallel to the seafront, past the Evergreen Café, restaurants and the tiny harbour. The tarmac ends near a supermarket but you continue past the Aquis Sandy Beach resort and across a bridged stream. Now veer left to head NW along the sand. You pass the lookout tower and café at **Issou beach** then a blue cabin and set your sights on the headland at the far end of the beautiful bay. However just before it, in the vicinity of clumps of large bushes (**20min** from Issou beach), turn right inland. You need to pick up the clear sandy piste used by quad bikers and walkers. It leads NW through low dunes colonised

Glorious Halikounas beach

Countess Lisl von Schlaf came to a nasty end on these very dunes in the 1981 James Bond film *For Your Eyes Only.*

by spreads of hardy flowers and windblown juniper shrubs. ◄ Further across you enter shady woodland of strawberry trees, myrtle and lentisc, to reach the lovely edge of Lake Korission. Follow this along to the footbridge (**1hr 15min**) across the Venetian-era channel to an old fisherman's hut populated by ravenous cats.

A wide lane now leads along the broad sand bar separating lake and sea. It's a leisurely stroll in the company of broom and juniper shrubs and showy sea daffodils, to the first of the attractive beachfront café-bars on beautiful **Halikounas beach** (**15min**).

After you've relaxed, swum, eaten and drunken your fill, retrace your steps to **Agios Georgios south** (**1hr 30min**).

WALK 19
Chlomos loop

Start/Finish	Roadside parking on the Linia–Chlomos road
Distance	4.5km
Ascent/Descent	150m/150m
Grade	1–2
Walking time	1hr 30min (45min extra on foot from Linia)
Refreshments	Linia, Chlomos
Access	From Linia on the main Lefkimmi–Corfu Town road take the minor road that branches N uphill opposite the café and turn-off for Issou/Issos. About 2km uphill after some bends, immediately following a gateway on the right to a house set back from the road, park on the roadside. On foot from the nearest bus stop – at Linia – allow 25min uphill (45min return time).

Set on a steep hillside overlooking beautiful Boukari bay and over to the Greek mainland, the delightful hill village of Chlomos is an attractive destination on this loop. The village centre, with its paved alleys and panoramic tavernas, is a precinct for pedestrians only.

The walk itself entails quite a few ups and downs but nothing especially strenuous, and trainers are fine as long as they have a good grip.

From the roadside take the lane left (NW at first) into an olive grove. It soon bears SW to a corner with vast views over the southern end of lovely Lake Korission. The way levels out and passes the gated drive to an isolated house before a minor dip. Very soon after a **tin shed** fork right uphill on a roughish rock track with a cypress tree on the corner for a short climb through spiny shrubs and then olive trees. As a wider lane is reached, branch right for a little more ascent and a glimpse of the east coast. A small **quarry** is the next useful landmark, while aerials can be seen ahead. Further on, a concrete lane leads out to a house on a surfaced road lined with cypress trees – turn

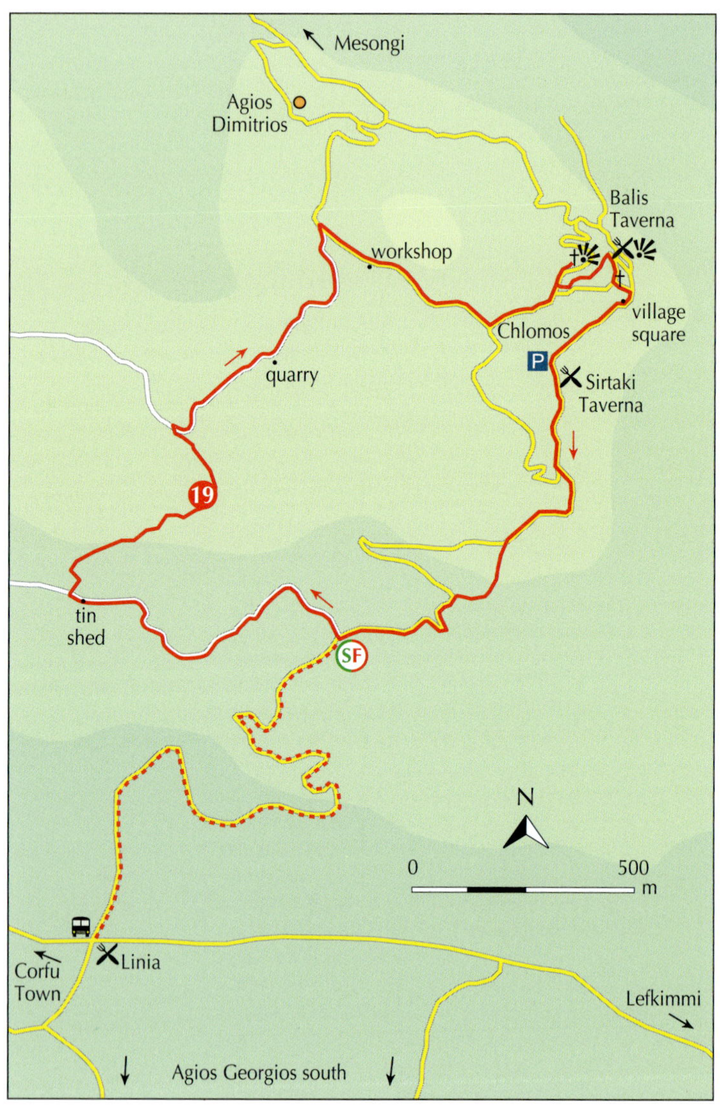

Mesongi
Agios Dimitrios
workshop
Balis Taverna
Chlomos
village square
quarry
Sirtaki Taverna
19
tin shed
SF
N
0
500
m
Corfu Town
Linia
Lefkimmi
Agios Georgios south

The panoramic church at Chlomos

right past a **workshop**. As you reach the edge of the village of **Chlomos**, take the road left. This quickly plunges past houses and an inviting craft shop to where a **church** perches, looking out over the village rooftops all the way to Lefkimmi and both east and west coasts.

Retrace your steps past a well and take the first alley left (signed for Sirtaki Taverna). Immaculately kept pastel coloured houses line the crazy-paved way. Follow the arrows left and down to another church alongside the **Balis Taverna** (**1hr**), a brilliantly panoramic spot for refreshments.

Turn right down a lane with crazy paving. At the next junction, go left then immediately right around a **church** (sign for 'Exit'). Several benches line the way then you keep right at a house with three columns. Next right is the triangular **village square**, a popular spot for the village inhabitants to pass the time of day. Left again leads out of the village and past cafés overlooking the hills. After a car park is the inviting, panoramic **Sirtaki Taverna**. At

The paved alleys of Chlomos

the next road junction branch left below an elongated derelict building. Not far along as the road bears right, leave it for a concrete-based lane descending left shortly before a road sign. A plunge through olive groves on a rough stony path ends at the road which is joined for the short remaining distance back to the roadside start point (**30min**).

WALK 20
The Lefkimmi Salt Pans

Start/Finish	Potami bridge
Distance	8.5km
Ascent/Descent	Negligible
Grade	1
Walking time	2hr 15min
Refreshments	Potami, Lefkimmi
Access	All buses on the Corfu Town–Kavos run stop on the bridge bus stop at Potami; car owners can park in one of the side streets nearby

If you enjoy dead flat land with vast expanses of still water, a backdrop of towering mountains on the Greek mainland, and aren't bothered by lack of shade, then this is the walk for you. Highlighted by landscapes where sunlight and clouds create a marvellous play of light and shadows across cracked salt-encrusted terrain and shallow lagoons, the Lefkimmi salt flats have undeniable charm. Salt was extracted here for centuries, and today the salt flats are an oasis for wildlife.

The walk's start, Potami, is attractive in its own right, a small village standing on the canal-like Himaros river, its banks lined with inviting cafés and tavernas. Sandals or trainers are fine for this walk, which is inadvisable in midsummer heat. Take plenty of drinking water – and binoculars for bird watching. Time permitting, it is possible to extend the walk by venturing further out on tracks along the edge of the salt pans towards the point.

From the bridge at **Potami**, with the **Himaros river** on your right, walk along the banks NNE in the direction of the sea. Passing the last houses, the narrow road becomes a waterside lane lined with tamarisk bushes. Further on, open flat land is reached near a little **harbour** where a fleet of tiny fishing boats is moored. Take the second lane left and proceed NNW in the company of stands of tall rushes, a couple of sheds and rows of magnificent eucalypts. A wide lane comes in from the left, but you

N
0
1
km
old salt pans
church
Alikes
pumping station
brick hut
circular building
lane crossroads
20
shrine
Convent of the Lady
harbour
Himaros river
Corfu Town
Lefkimmi
Potami
bridge
SF

keep straight on at the junction. ▸ A batch of solar panels precede an abandoned **circular building** with a curious white cone on its roof. The main lane soon veers left but you leave it for a lesser lane straight ahead, in the direction of a ruined building. This turns out to be a rusting **pumping station**, set on a channel on the edge of the salt pans, a marvellous spot.

This stretch gives extensive views over the sea to the Greek mainland.

Sea water was left at length in shallow open **salt pans** to evaporate, then hauled by horse to the old salt works. Salt was essential for preserving foodstuffs for transport by sea, and the Venetians had a monopoly. Operations date all the way back to the 1400s and the centuries-long activity was only brought to a halt in 1988.

Nowadays rusting machinery stands witness among what has become an important wetlands

The path across the old salt pans

site and breeding haven for birds, both migratory and non-migratory, including waders herons, oystercatchers, seagulls and even flamingos. A bonus is the interesting range of plant life and flowers that thrive in this salty habitat.

Now bear left (SW) on a wide sandy lane in a straight line among glasswort and sea lavender plants, to a derelict **brick hut**. Branch right here for a fascinating crossing between shallow salt flats, some dried up, and others alive with seagulls and egrets who use worn pole stubs as perches for fishing. ◄ Back on solid ground are a **church** and long stone building, once a salt warehouse. Close-by is small harbour. Turn left onto the road alongside picnic tables belonging to the modest beach of **Alikes** (**1hr 15min**).

As the houses start, take the first road turning left, which soon becomes a broad lane. About 500m in, as it shows signs of curving left (NE), leave it for a branch right (SE) under power lines heading away from the sea. Stick with this on a grassy stretch through olive groves and past properties. At a **crossroads of lanes** fork right (S) in the shade of tall trees, continuing on to a Y-fork and a red-and-white **shrine**. It's not far on until you emerge at tarmac, houses and the **Convent of the Lady**. Turn right (S) down the road to **Lefkimmi** (bus stop, shops, café). By turning left here the walk loop can be completed with a return to the **Potami bridge** (**1hr**).

Towards the far end on a sand spit a batch of old machinery lies rusting in the undergrowth, witness to a long-gone activity.

The main road is reached at Lefkimmi

WALK 21

Arkoudilas beach circuit

Start/Finish	Kavos bus stop
Distance	9km
Ascent/Descent	200m/200m
Grade	2
Walking time	2hr 45min
Refreshments	Nothing en route
Access	The terminus for the Green Bus line is located at a Y-intersection near the Alpha Bank

Leaving Kavos and its buzz far behind, partly following the opening stage of the Corfu Trail, this route heads towards the island's southernmost headland. It drops in on the quiet modest beach of Arkoudilas at the foot of brooding eroded cliffs, where walkers need to be prepared to take off boots and socks if the tide is in. After a steep scenic climb and a jaunt through a rural landscape the circuit concludes back at Kavos. Carry drinking water and a picnic, as well as swimming gear and sun protection.

The route can be extended – by 30min – via the ruined Monastery of Arkoulidas, or shortened by returning the quick way – see Walk 22.

From the Kavos bus stop don't head for the beach, but instead go right (SE) and past The Steak House restaurant. Further along you pass playing grounds and the Miami Hotel before reaching the **Kavos Plaza** Hotel. Turn right along this road then turn left at the next intersection (where the return route comes out) in the direction of **Asprocavos**. But very soon be prepared to leave the tarmac for a lane right (S) recognisable for the black/yellow Corfu Trail symbol as well as a sign for a monastery. This leads past rural properties with orchards and ancient olive trees.

Over a rise the lane forks – left goes to the **Monastery of Arkoudilas**: keep straight ahead (SW) for the gentle descent to **Arkoudilas beach** (**45min**). ▶ Go right along

This is a lovely quiet if narrow strip of sand looking over to the island of Paxi.

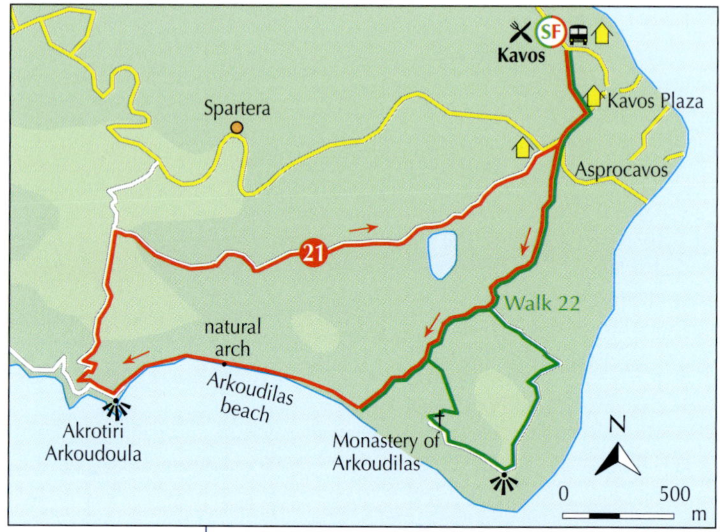

the seafront, which is strewn with large pebbles, to a stretch below eroding cliffs. Depending on the tides, you may or may not be dodging waves. Near the end of the beach is a small **natural arch**, a gap between giant toes on a monstrous animal paw – walkers need to duck through if the tide is in. Watch out for waves!

Soon comes a tricky clamber over banks of seaweed and up a high, badly eroded bank to join a concreted lane. This climbs steeply in wide curves for an excellent outlook over the **Akrotiri Arkoudoula** headland. But don't miss the first fork right for the drawn-out uphill slog N amidst flowering bushes and dizzy coast views. Stick with the lane as it levels out through olive groves. About 1km from the beach and just before a rise, branch right on a clear lane. With gentle dips this leads mostly E through woodland and olive farms. Ignore turn-offs. Touching on a sizeable lake, the lane proceeds NE. It eventually passes a villa and hotel, joins the road from **Spartera** and is soon at the **Asprocavos** intersection passed earlier on. Keep straight ahead to return to **Kavos** (**2hr**).

WALK 22

The Short Arkoudilas loop

Start/Finish	Kavos bus stop
Distance	7.5km
Ascent/Descent	150m/150m
Grade	1–2
Walking time	2hr
Refreshments	Nothing en route
Access	The terminus for the Green Bus line is located at a Y-intersection near the Alpha Bank

This is a short jaunt through woodland via a crumbling 18th-century monastery on a panoramic cliff-top, to a quiet if narrow beach close to the island's southeastern point. Water, sun protection and swimming things are in order. For a longer version of this route see Walk 21.

From the Kavos bus stop don't head for the beach, but instead go right (SE) and past The Steak House restaurant. Further along you pass playing grounds and the Miami Hotel before reaching the **Kavos Plaza** Hotel. Turn right along this road then turn left at the next intersection (where the return route comes out) in the direction of **Asprocavos**. But very soon be prepared to leave the tarmac for a lane right (S) recognisable for the black/yellow Corfu Trail symbol as well as a sign for a monastery. This leads past rural properties with orchards and ancient olive trees.

Over a rise the way forks – keep left (SE) in common with the CT for a gentle climb to a panoramic corner which unfortunately doubles as a rubbish dump. Thereafter you're accompanied by masses of Mediterranean bushes and lovely views over the Ionian Sea from what is the southernmost coast of Corfu. At the end of the lane stands what's left of the **Monastery of Arkoudilas** (100m).

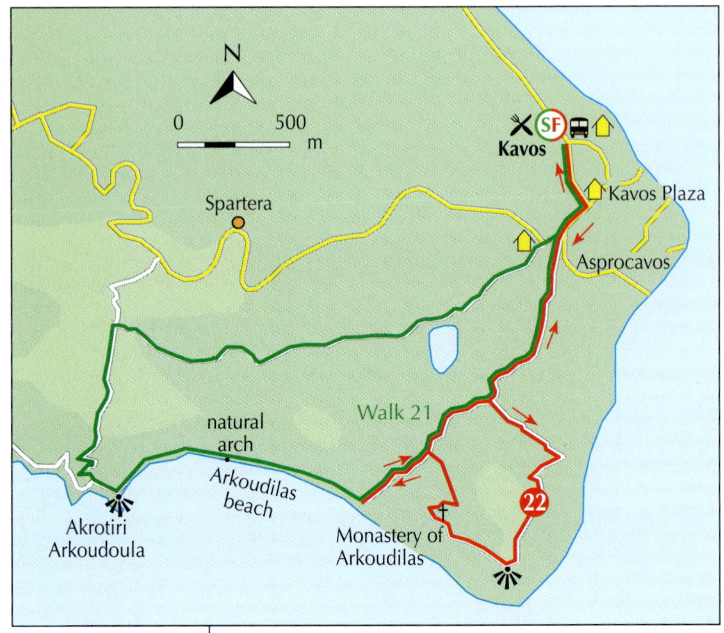

On the left of the buildings a clear path begins its descent through woodland, rather precipitous in places. ◄ A stream crossing precedes a steep but short climb to a lane. Turn left here for the short descent to **Arkoudilas beach** (**1hr 15min**).

Watch your step if the ground is wet as it can be slippery.

This is a lovely and quiet, if narrow, **strip of sand** looking over to the island of Paxi. The seafront is strewn with large pebbles and dominated by eroding cliffs.

The return route takes the lane you arrived on, but instead of following the detour via the monastery, stays on the lane that climbs gently to rejoin the outward route at the lane fork. From there you retrace your steps back to the road then **Kavos** (**45min**).

Mirtiotissas beach is glimpsed during the descent route on Stage 6

Corfu Trail
Agios Spiridonas
F
Aharavi
Kassiopi
Old Perithia
Mount Pandokratoras
Sokraki
Barbati
Agios Georgios nth
Liapades beach
Corfu Town
Kavos
4h 15min
Potami
4h 30min
Agios Georgios south
4h 15min
Paramonas
4h 30min
Dafnata
5h 30min
Pelekas
6h
Liapades beach
3h 15min
Agios Georgios north
Pelekas
Benitses
Dafnata
Paramonas
Mesongi
Agios Georgios north
5h 40min
Sokraki
5h
Old Perithia
3h 30min
Agios Spiridonas
Agios Georgios sth
Potami
S
N
0   10 km

A divine sunset from Pelekas onto Agios Georgios mountain

The Corfu Trail (CT), a 150km (93 mile) trek exploring Corfu from far south to far north, was devised in 2001 by a group of Corfu residents including Hilary Paipeti, whose work in encouraging walking on the island is praiseworthy. The trail begins at the island's southeasternmost tip, near Kavos, and touches a clutch of long sandy beaches and magnificent Lake Korission before looping inland to hospitable hill villages and belvedere-like settlement of Pelekas. A traverse of the lush agricultural Ropa valley plain is followed by stretches along the magnificent rocky coast around Paleokastritsa and Agios Georgios north. The CT then veers east inland to climb the rugged slopes of Mount Pandokratoras before a superb conclusion on Corfu's northerly promontory at Agios Spiridonas.

Waymarks – which are not that frequent – are yellow metal plaques marked with 'CT' and black arrows. Painted yellow arrows or blotches are also encountered at irregular intervals, but these may easily be confused with the lemon-tinted lichens that colonise many a tree and rock. Some strategic points are marked by cairns, small heaps of stones left by other walkers to show the way. The route description is purposely detailed to make up for the dearth of waymarking.

The starting point to this exciting trek is Kavos (or Cavos), close to the island's far southeastern tip, and a curious place. There is no village as such, but parallel to an attractive long sandy beach is a high street straight out of a Western film, with shoulder-to-shoulder shops, restaurants and bars with a reputation for night-long partying throughout the midsummer months. However it's sleepy and quiet enough in spring and late summer, when most walkers will be passing through. Accommodation options include friendly Rantos Apartments B&B, tel 26620 61361 mob 6948 572957 www.rantosapartments.com; San Marina Hotel tel 26620 61345 www.corfusanmarina.com. Buses from Corfu Town come this far and there's an ATM.

STAGE 1
Kavos to Potami

Start	Kavos bus stop
Distance	14km
Ascent	230m
Descent	230m
Grade	2
Walking time	4hr 15min
Refreshments	Spartera, Potami

This excellent opening stage to the Corfu Trail leaves the popular beach resort of Kavos via a crumbling 18th-century monastery on a cliff top. After a plunge through woodland comes a quiet beach at the foot of brooding eroded cliffs. A steep climb leads to a belvedere hamlet followed by a wander through olive groves to photogenic Potami. On a canal-like river not far from the eastern coast, this is one of the string of six laid-back, connected villages that comprise Lefkimmi, Corfu's second largest settlement.

Allow a full day for this stage as it is surprisingly tiring.

From the Kavos bus stop (the terminus for the Green Bus line) at the Y-fork in the road with the Alpha Bank, don't proceed towards the beach but go right (SE) and past The Steak House restaurant. Further along you pass playing grounds and the Miami Hotel before reaching the Kavos Plaza Hotel. Turn right along this road then left at the next intersection in the direction of **Asprocavos**, but very soon leave the tarmac for a lane right (S) recognisable for the black/yellow Corfu Trail symbol as well as a sign for a monastery. This leads past rural properties and ancient olive trees. Over a rise the way forks, the CT going left (SE) for a gentle climb to a **panoramic corner** which unfortunately doubles as a rubbish dump. ◄ The lane concludes at what's left of the **Monastery of Arkoudilas** (100m, **50min**).

From here on the way is accompanied by masses of Mediterranean bushes and lovely views over the Ionian Sea from what is the southernmost coast of Corfu.

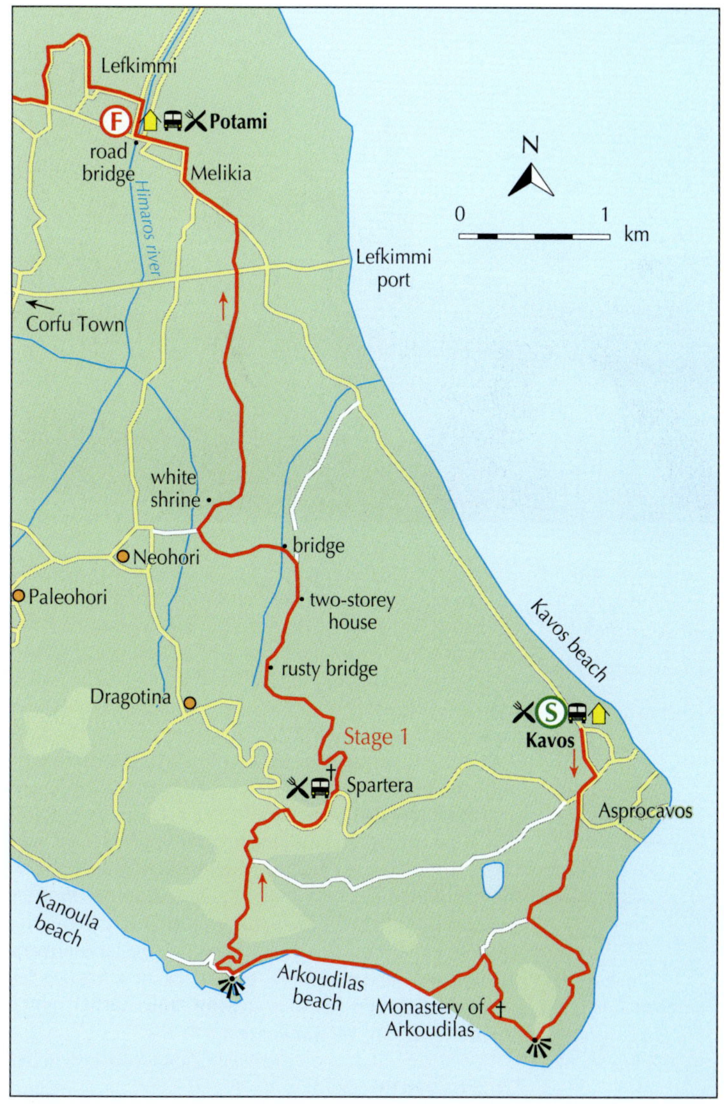

Lefkimmi
Potami
road bridge
Melikia
Himaros river
Lefkimmi port
N
0 1 km
Corfu Town
white shrine
bridge
Neohori
two-storey house
Paleohori
rusty bridge
Kavos beach
Dragotina
Stage 1
Kavos
Spartera
Asprocavos
Kanoula beach
Arkoudilas beach
Monastery of Arkoudilas

The CT visits the ruins of Arkoudilas monastery

There are vast views to the Greek mainland.

On the left of the buildings a clear path begins its descent through woodland, precipitous in places. After crossing a stream it climbs steeply but briefly to a lane. Go left here for **Arkoudilas beach** (**25min**). Turn right to follow the lovely strip of sand looking over to the island of Paxi. The seafront is strewn with large pebbles and dominated by eroding cliffs. Depending on the tides, you may or may not be dodging waves so be prepared to take off your boots.

Near the end of the beach after a natural arch under what resembles a giant animal paw, you clamber over banks of seaweed and up a high, badly eroded bank to join a concreted lane that climbs steeply. Don't miss the first fork right for the uphill slog N amidst flowering bushes and dizzy coast **views**. Stick with the lane through olive groves and over a rise. Up at a surfaced road you're pointed right past the bus stop for the quiet village of **Spartera** (130m, **1hr 15min**). ◀

At the Bellavista Café leave the main road and go left to the attractive yellow church and its massive ancient olive tree. Immediately after the building turn left to pass the cemetery on a descending concreted lane. Veer right at the bottom through olive groves to join a white stony lane near a pylon. Branch left then soon at a T-junction go right. Ignoring turn-offs continue on over a **bridge with rusty railings** and on past vegetable gardens and a miniature **two-storey house**. Only minutes along, the CT branches left to cross an overgrown **bridge**. This lane proceeds mostly W through shady olive groves of ancient and not-so-old trees. At the next junction go right onto a gravel lane downhill to where a CT sign points you right. This way quickly curves right near a tiny **white shrine**, then soon it's left over a rise for a lengthy stretch due N along net fencing. Eventually you reach the main Corfu Town–**Lefkimmi port** road. Cross straight over with due care and walk along the continuation of the lane through to another road which you follow left (W) through **Melikia**, part of Lefkimmi. Not far along is **Potami** (**1hr 45min**) and the **road bridge** across the canal-like **Himaros river.**

Once important for transporting goods to the coast, the **Himaros river** is now lined with inviting tavernas. 'Potami' actually means 'river'.

Accommodation is available either at River Restaurant (go right before the bridge and follow the quayside) tel 26620 24032 mob 6974 613677, or Rooms to let (turn left after the bridge, mob 6945 973779). There is bus access and groceries.

STAGE 2
Potami to Agios Georgios south

Start	Road bridge at Potami
Distance	15km
Ascent	160m
Descent	160m
Grade	2
Walking time	4hr 30min
Refreshments	Lefkimmi, Gardenos, Santa Barbara, Agios Georgios south

This is a varied stage that sees the CT wending its way through the maze of Lefkimmi, with its countless churches, before embarking on a traverse from the east coast via the rural valley of the Gardenos river. Then it's over a headland to reach Corfu's glorious southwest, with vast golden beaches and the low-key beach resort of Agios Georgios south. Well-deserved swims can be enjoyed along the way thanks to a long spell along the sand.

Several alternative accommodation options are passed en route.

Cross the road bridge at **Potami** and turn right past the riverside cafés. Take the third little street on the left (at the bins) through to crossroads and go right. At the ensuing T-junction go left and through to the main road which you follow right (cafés, groceries, bus stop immediately left). The 16th century church of the **Blessed Virgin Odigitria** is passed and you continue on through the built-up area of **Lefkimmi**. Further on ignore the road fork right for Molos, but immediately after a large church with twin bell towers, you need the first left between cafés. Follow this narrow side road as it leads down to a square at the rear of yet another church, this one with double white bell towers and a curved raised stone wall. ◄

Lovely views over the island's south and the mainland can be enjoyed here.

Keep straight ahead past houses and as things begin to look more countrified, keep an eye out for a fork right signposted for Corfu. This leads downhill to a bigger road where you go left past rural properties and villas to a

Corfu Town
Kaliviotis beach
Griti beach
Molos
Blessed Virgin Odigitria
Map continues on page 132
Perivoli
Lefkimmi
Potami
Santa Barbara
Vitalades
main intersection
petrol station
Lefkimmi port
Himaros river
shrine
Y-junction
Gardenos river
T-junction
Stage 2
Neohori
Gardenos
Gardenos beach
Kritika
Paleohori
N
0
1
km

main intersection on the Lefkimmi port–Corfu Town road (**50min**). Cross with care and take the road for Kritika S past a **petrol station**. After a bridge the CT takes the first turning right at a house and corner **shrine**. This unmade road heads SW through open countryside with olive groves. After a batch of solar panels and a fenced farm keep right at a Y fork towards a power pylon. Gentle descent leads through thickly woodland, past a farm and vegetable gardens, ending up at a minor road. You turn right to cross the **Gardenos** river and quickly reach a T-junction with a taverna. Go left (SSW) in the direction of the sea as far as the Alexandros Taverna (rooms mob 6976 215429) at **Gardenos** (**1hr**).

Immediately before the buildings take the steep concrete lane that climbs to the rear of the taverna and up past tiny farms. It becomes a dirt lane passing old low farmers huts made of local sandstone bricks. Continue uphill to where the lane divides and veer left in the company of goats, vineyards and vast views. Heading NNW it finally levels out in olive groves. After a house with massive concrete foundations it swings right looking over to the east coast and mainland. Soon at a **T-junction** go left uphill briefly then swing right again (SW) at the next fork through fields of grapes and olives. Stay with this clear lane leading mostly W through Mediterranean bush.

Soon after the second of two intersections branch left in descent on a concrete lane to a strategic **Y-junction** with gorgeous views to the beaches and lake ahead. Now it's left again on a brilliantly scenic sandy lane NW on the cliff edge. At a saddle take the rough track sharp left down to the beach at last! With or without your boots on, make your way along the golden sand at the foot

The CT winds in and out of streets at Lefkimmi

133

of eroding cliffs, to laid back **Santa Barbara** aka Agia Varvara (**1hr 30min**, cafés, restaurants and Maria Rooms tel 26620 23151 **www.corfusantabarbara.com**).

Splash or jump across the modest river that flows into the sea here and keep along the sand where stands of reeds spill down from gullies. Further along, where a tricky **rock outcrop** invades the beach, take the short rough path up to a good lane along the cliff top. Passing vegetable gardens and the odd house, the lane becomes surfaced and reaches a great belvedere taverna that marks the beginning of the spread-out resort of Agios Georgios south. Not far on are Barbayannis rooms and restaurant. The road proceeds parallel to the inviting seafront, past a small church and supermarket, bus stops and the Blue Sea Hotel, to the end of the road at **Agios Georgios south** (**1hr 10min**) with cafés and restaurants.

AGIOS GEORGIOS SOUTH AND NORTH

This Agios Georgios has been given the tag 'south' for the purposes of this guide to distinguish it from the northern location: Agios Georgios south is sometimes referred to as Agios Georgios Argyrades.

The many accommodation options include Barbayannis (tel 26620 52110) and the friendly Blue Sea Hotel (tel 26620 51624 **www.bluesea-hotel.com**).

STAGE 3

Agios Georgios south to Paramonas

Start	Agios Georgios south
Distance	15km
Ascent	100m
Descent	80m
Grade	2
Walking time	4hr 15min
Refreshments	Issou, Halikounas beach, Alonaki Bay, Paramonas

Sandy beaches, flower-smothered dunes and placid Lake Korission, which is home to water fowl, make for a magnificent start to this stage. By all means walk the opening section in sandals. The latter part is on quiet inland roads shaded by olive trees on the slopes of Prasoudi mountain before the conclusion at Paramonas and a small beach. Waymarking is sorely lacking throughout so follow directions carefully. Alonaki Bay is a lovely alternative place to stay en route.

From the western end of **Agios Georgios south**, where the main road turns inland, keep straight ahead parallel to the seafront past cafés, restaurants and a supermarket to the end of the tarmac. Walk past the Aquis Sandy Beach

The lookout tower and beach at Issou

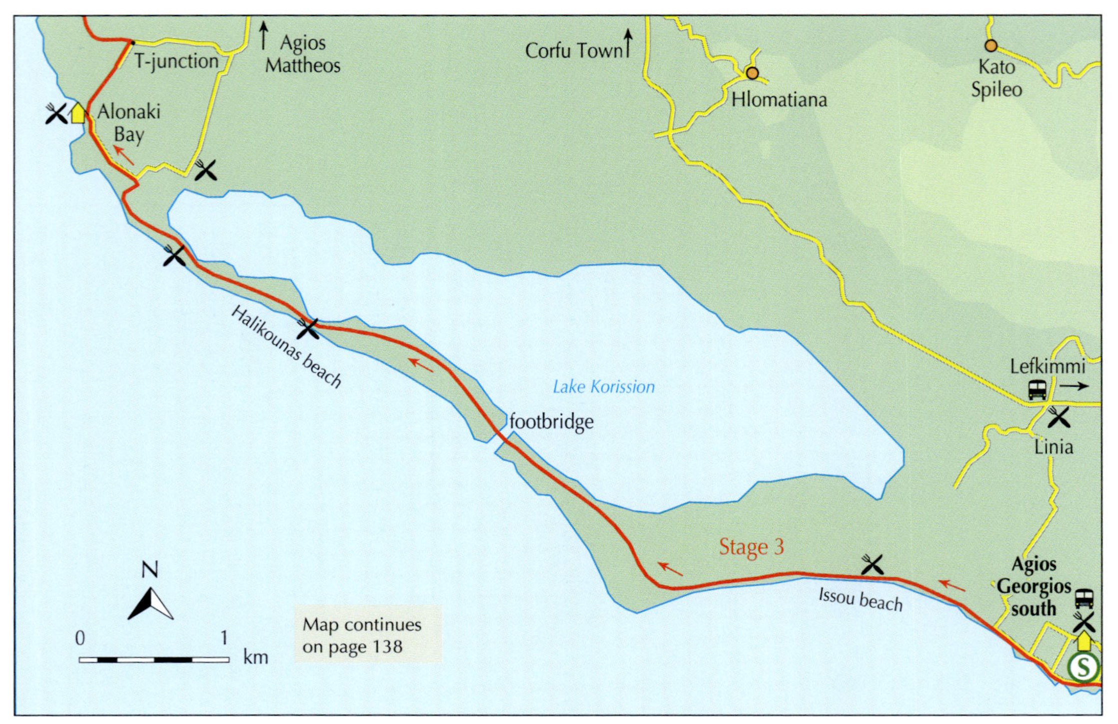

T-junction
Agios Mattheos
Corfu Town
Hlomatiana
Kato Spileo
Alonaki Bay
Halikounas beach
Lake Korission
footbridge
Lefkimmi
Linia
Stage 3
Issou beach
Agios Georgios south
N
0
1
km
Map continues on page 138

resort and across a bridged stream. Now veer left to head NW along the seafront. You pass the lookout tower and café at **Issou beach** (also referred to as Issos), then a blue cabin. Set your sights on the headland at the far end of the beautiful bay, however just before it, in the vicinity of clumps of large bushes (**20min** from Issou beach), turn right inland. Here a clear sandy piste used by quad bikers and walkers leads NW through low dunes. ▶ Further across you enter shady woodland of strawberry trees, myrtle and lentisc, and reach the edge of lovely **Lake Korission**, with views to Prasoudi mountain. Follow this to a **footbridge** (**1hr 15min**) across a channel, cut through to the sea in Venetian times when the lake was used for fish breeding. Over the other side is an old fisherman's hut populated by ravenous cats.

In the company of a brilliant palette of colourful wildflowers, a wide lane now leads along the consolidated sand bar separating the lake from the sea and beautiful **Halikounas beach**. Stroll past a couple of attractive

The piste across the sand dunes towards Lake Korission

The dunes are colonised by spreads of hardy flowers and windblown juniper shrubs.

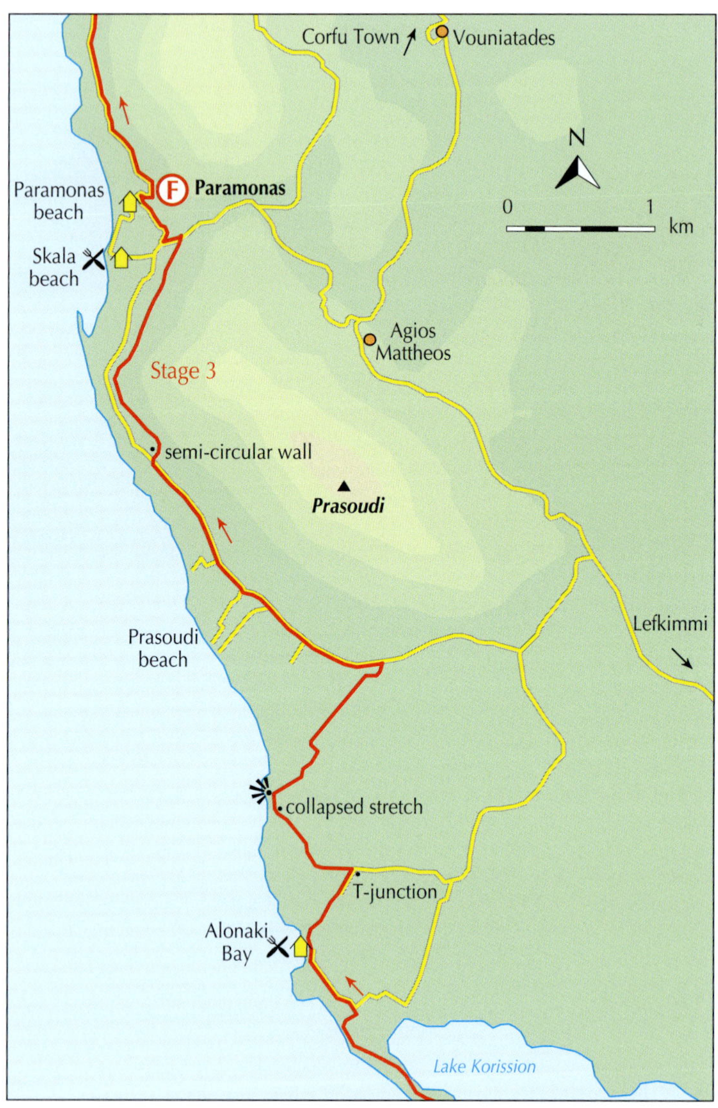

Corfu Town
Vouniatades
N
0
1
km
Paramonas beach
F Paramonas
Skala beach
Agios Mattheos
Stage 3
semi-circular wall
Prasoudi
Lefkimmi
Prasoudi beach
collapsed stretch
T-junction
Alonaki Bay
Lake Korission

beachfront café-bars to the end of the lake and keep straight ahead, cutting across a small headland. After veering right to a minor surfaced road, go left past fields to the fork (**50min**) for **Alonaki Bay** Taverna (tel 26610 75872), but unless you desire lunch or a room keep straight on the unmade lane that turns inland through olive groves. After a minor landfill site the way is surfaced again. At a **T-junction** and villas the CT branches left back to the sea edge where the road is closed to motorised traffic due to a short **collapsed stretch** – however walkers can proceed on a narrow clifftop path.

This quickly leads to picnic tables and a **lookout** with lovely views up the northwestern coast and island outcrops at the foot of Prasoudi mountain. Now the road bears NE inland to join a larger road left (NW) passing monstrously ancient olive trees. Further on houses and beach turn-offs are passed before a gentle uphill section leads to a curious high semi-circular wall of old stones on the right. Here the CT finally parts way with the tarmac, branching right uphill on a lane, which soon bears L to coast through olive terraces for a longish relaxing stroll mostly N. Further on at a road you go left.

If you're staying at the comfortable Paramonas Hotel at Skala beach then stay with the road to where it points right for the seafront: tel 26610 76595 **www.paramonas-hotel.com**.

Otherwise fork immediately right uphill until you reach the **Paramonas beach** turn-off (**2hr 10min**) with a cluster of signs.

Close-by on the left are simple rooms to let (Varagulis Giannis tel 26610 76702 or 26610 36434). There's a restaurant down at the beach.

STAGE 4
Paramonas to Dafnata

Start	Paramonas beach turn-off
Distance	14km
Ascent	620m
Descent	340m
Grade	2
Walking time	4hr 40min
Refreshments	Ano Pavliana, Kato Pavliana, Strongili, Dafnata

After heading steeply up and over a panoramic ridge the CT loops decidedly inland through a string of quiet villages and rural landscapes, crossing the island almost to the eastern coast. The day's conclusion is the lofty village of Dafnata, boasting marvellous views over Corfu Town and its bay.

From the **Paramonas beach turn-off** walk up the road past villas and rural properties for around **8min** to a corner where the CT is pointed up sharp R. It takes a narrow steep concreted path with abundant yellow markings and arrows. After a house it's straight uphill past huts and olive terraces. The steady climb leads through vegetable plots, and there are lovely views back down to Paramonas beach. The way becomes an old path that proceeds NNE through Mediterranean shrubs and herbs with odd overgrown stretches. A wide track is joined near a **belvedere corner** (280m) looking up Corfu's magnificent northwest coast. The climb continues past light grey outcrops and broom spattered mountainside, to reach a level dirt road. This quickly leads through a minor **pass** (350m). ◄

Here are with sweeping views, now over the east coast.

Down at a junction the CT goes right, but is soon pointed left before a house onto a rough path into shrubs. Further down at a house a plunging concreted road takes over. Keep right at a fork to a tiny pretty square shaded by an enormous lime tree. A sharp right will see you down at the road in **Ano Pavliana** (275m, **1hr 20min**, café and shop).

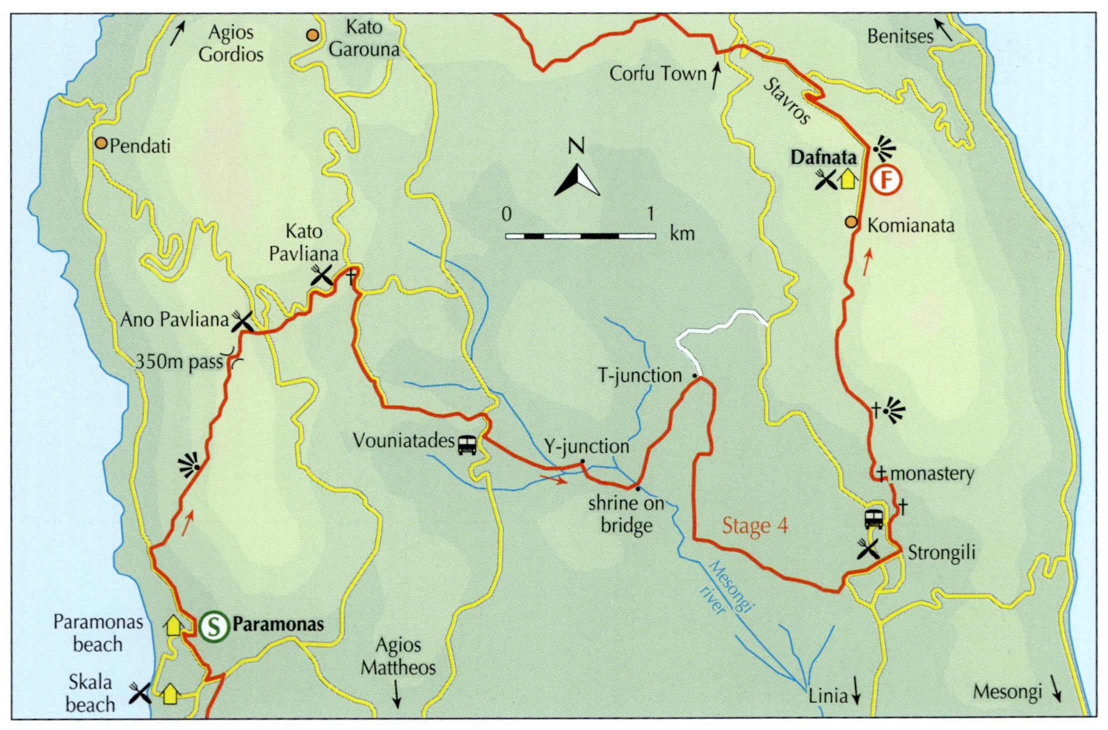

Agios Gordios
Kato Garouna
Benitses
Corfu Town
Stavros
Pendati
Dafnata
F
Komianata
Kato Pavliana
N
0   1   km
Ano Pavliana
350m pass
T-junction
monastery
Vouniatades
Y-junction
shrine on bridge
Stage 4
Strongili
Paramonas beach
S Paramonas
Agios Mattheos
Mesongi river
Skala beach
Linia
Mesongi

The path down to Ano Pavliana

The CT originally turned off right before a batch of letterboxes but this route is impassable as it is grossly overgrown.

Turn right, then only minutes downhill left for a descending path NNE through vegetable plots then trees. There are three stream crossings before you curve up to a road – go right past houses and a café in **Kato Pavliana** (215m) and stick to the road. ◄ Proceed as far as the church and branch right, still on tarmac. Further down, immediately after Villa Romantica take the minor road right for a quiet descent mostly S through olive groves, then dipping across a valley planted with grapes. After a bridge the road climbs to a junction on a rise – fork left (E) on a lane leading out to the road at **Vouniatades** and a bus stop (**1hr**).

Following CT markers carefully, turn right then first left between houses along the first of several paved alleys, as you continue dropping to a quiet road. Here go left (E) past rural properties on what is soon a lane. A concrete bridge crosses a stream and it's on beneath huge shady olive trees to a **Y-junction**. Fork right over another bridge and follow this lane as far as a **shrine on a bridge**, where you cross left over the modest **Mesongi river**. A lovely stroll NNE ensues through low-lying bushy vegetation with lentisc, asphodels and myriad orchids. At a **T-junction** go right for a long level stretch mostly S then ESE past olive groves and sheep and goats at pasture. After a playing field the way is surfaced and leads through to **Strongili** (40m, **1hr**, friendly taverna, cafés and groceries).

The CT crosses straight over the Corfu Town–Mesongi road, through to minor crossroads and the village square where you fork left to the main road again. Here it's right past a bus shelter and a map board and you take the second right, a concreted lane uphill to a **church** with inviting benches. A rough track continues past the grave-yard, and you soon fork right gently uphill through olive groves. Where a rusty gate is detoured you spy the white buildings of a modest **monastery** on your left beneath rocky mountain flanks.

The CT now follows a curious short loop, drop-ping past the building to a stepped path down through a lemon orchard. At a lane turn right and climb up past huts to follow yellow metal poles and a faint path. An overgrown but clear lane is joined – follow it right up to another tiny **church** with a lovely view to the Agii Deka. Continue in gentle ascent N through olive groves which give way to bushland dominated by masses of rock roses then scented broom. Just after a bunch of skeletal trees are huts and vegetable plots then the tiny mountainside hamlet of **Komianata**. On your right is the minuscule square. Take the next left past houses to quickly reach the road. A short way along is the day's conclusion, the mountain village of **Dafnata** (320m, **1hr 20min**).

Dafnata is one of the clusters of houses that come under the collective name of Stavros. It boasts great views over Corfu Town and to the Agii Deka moun-tain, traversed in Stage 5 and recognisable for its giant golf ball-cum-radar device.

As well as an authentic red telephone box, there's a friendly café-taverna with rooms (Kostas Raris tel 26610 57345 mob 6946 471449 kosraris@yahoo.gr. Accommodation also at The Olive Press tel 26610 57307.)

STAGE 5
Dafnata to Pelekas

Start	Kostas Taverna, Dafnata
Distance	17km
Ascent	600m
Descent	700m
Grade	2
Walking time	5hr 30min
Refreshments	Makrata, Sinarades, Pelekas

A strenuous but rewarding day, with much ascent and descent. The lovely start crosses Agii Deka, 'ten saints' mountain, often referred to, on account of its peaceful monastery, as Pantokrator, or Christ depicted as Almighty ruler of the universe. Confusingly, the name is almost identical to that of Corfu's principal peak, Oros Pandokratoras.

The route then heads downhill to touch on a string of villages, including well-served Sinarades. A scenic path above the coast precedes a lengthy inland stretch through olive groves: all ends happily at Pelekas, an attractive mountaintop village sitting high over the west coast and well adjusted to tourist needs. There are no intermediate accommodation options on this long stage: one way to shorten it would be to take a bus from Sinarades to Corfu Town then another bus out to Pelekas.

Leave **Dafnata** (320m) on the panoramic road-cum-ridge heading mostly NW down past the succession of houses and churches that make up **Stavros**. You emerge on the Corfu Town–Strongili road at **Makrata** (250m, **15min**, café on the left). Cross straight over for a quiet concrete-based road signposted for Pantokrator. After a shrine then a **chapel**, it's gently uphill past a field where you branch left off the road at a brick wall. Heading W this quickly narrows to a clear path crossing streams in damp woodland, and wandering past pencil-straight cypresses and through long-abandoned olive groves where stone terraces are thick with moss. Well marked, the way continues past

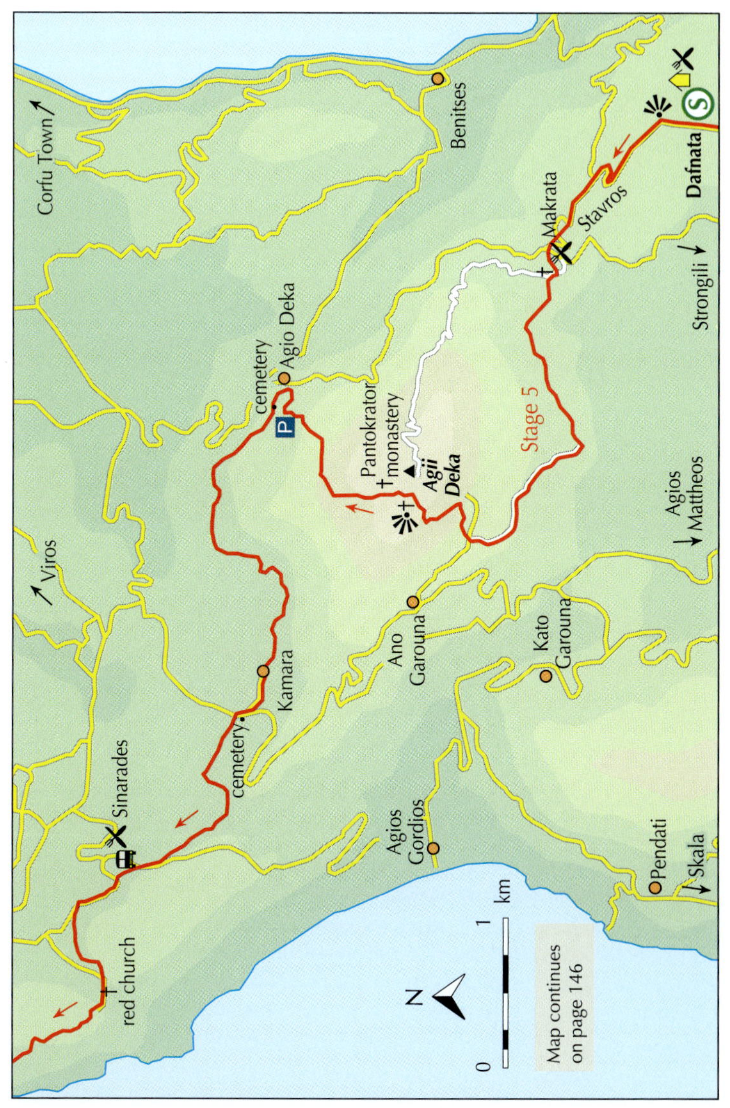

Corfu Town
Benitses
Dafnata
Strongili
Makrata
Stavros
Agio Deka
cemetery
P
Pantokrator monastery
Agii Deka
Stage 5
Agios Mattheos
Viros
Kamara
cemetery
Ano Garouna
Kato Garouna
Sinarades
Agios Gordios
Pendati
Skala
red church
N
km
1
0
Map continues on page 146

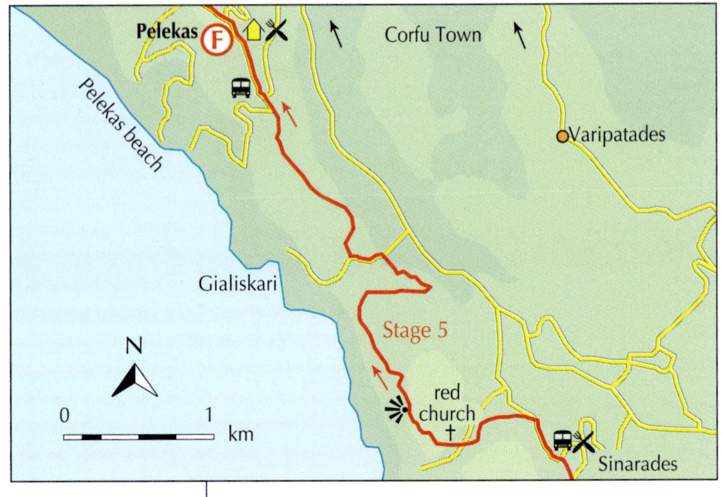

huge boulders of pebble conglomerate, the atmosphere reminiscent of a ghost village. A lane takes over to lead past scattered huts under olive trees, climbing gently but steadily WNW as views open up.

At houses and a minor road go left then first right to pick up a narrow path. After a short level stretch, brace yourself for a stiff climb winding mostly NW over olive terraces. A flatter section crosses ivy-smothered wood before a steeper bit that concludes at a whitewashed chapel in a marvellously panoramic clearing on the edge of the **Agii Deka** mountain, with the giant radar golf ball visible to the northeast. Head down the lane and keep left for the **Pantokrator monastery** (530m, **1hr 30min**) with a peaceful garden shaded by spreading trees. ◀

Leave the premises by way of a gate (left) onto a path along a stone wall and orchard and N into a wood. As the descent begins, take the right fork for Agio Deka on a knee-jarring path that affords plenty of opportunities for admiring the coastline and Corfu Town. About half an hour from the top a lane is reached and you go left down steep concreted ramps. A marked path to the

> Don't miss the church with its wonderful painting of Pantokrator, Christ the Almighty.

right ends at a car park. Here the CT veers right along a paved alley past old buildings to a bell tower. Keep right and follow the yellow markers past another church to the road at **Agio Deka** village (220m, **45min**). Go left past a children's playground to a Y-intersection, and continue straight ahead NW past a large **cemetery**. The path becomes a lane with minor ups and downs, alternating wood and olive groves below sheer rock outcrops and masses of cypresses. Ignore a fork near an ornate gate and continue on to houses before a yellow mansion – turn right for a pretty paved square, then follow the minor road left. Further along are villas and an ample car park, and soon you encounter the tiny square of **Kamara**. ▶

Drinking water is available here.

Keep left around the orange-tinted church along an alley and soon right down a stepped path that dips across a stream. Up at a road go right for a short distance past a shrine and **cemetery** and immediately afterwards leave the tarmac for a path left along a wire fence. Further on this widens. At a lane crossroads branch left

This shrine and cemetery are a handy landmark between Kamara and Sinarades

uphill flanking a fenced citrus orchard which gives way to woodland. Keep right at the next junction and along to meet a lane, then it's right into olive groves. You emerge on a busy road where the CT goes right towards houses, but very soon a concreted lane branches off left and you follow yellow signs past the Folk Museum and towards the church tower. Keep left past a taverna to the square of **Sinarades** (**1hr 10min**, groceries, cafés, bus stop). ◄

This is a good place for lunch, and you're over halfway now!

Continue on past a smaller square. As the road bears right, the CT branches left onto a paved alley to weave its way past tiny old houses. A concreted lane leads up past a newer house then goes sharp right, and is soon surfaced. At a T-junction cross straight over and up past a tiny **red church**. Here keep left through scented broom bushes on a lane high over the beautiful west coast; not far on is an especially **panoramic corner**.

At a T-junction keep left for a mostly level section N before another veer inland in descent. At the bottom of the slope it's left for a seemingly never-ending loop parallel to the road at times. ◄ On finally reaching houses and a surfaced road go left to flank the high wall of a private property. As the road bears left (for **Gialiskari**), the CT parts ways with it to fork right, resuming the N direction parallel to and above a road, looking inland. Further on a shrine then a wall are passed before you emerge at a road. Follow this in ascent past a bus stop for the final climb of the day, concluding at the attractive hilltop village of **Pelekas** (240m, **1hr 50min**).

Curiously it feels as if you're backtracking.

Once rested go for an exploratory wander around the old traffic-free village and find the energy to venture up to the highest point, which boasts the famous **Emperor's Throne lookout**, not to be missed. The café-restaurant terrace up top is perfect for sunset.

Pelekas offers groceries, cafés and buses. Alongside the main square is budget Agnes Rooms tel 26610 94997 **www.agnespelekas.com**, whereas further uphill is Jimmy's Restaurant and Rooms tel 26610 94284 mob 6973 596644 **www.jimmyspelekas.com**.

Start	Pelekas square
Distance	22.5km
Ascent	500m
Descent	700m
Grade	2
Walking time	6hr
Refreshments	Mirtiotissas beach, Kellia, Vatos, Giannades, Liapades, Liapades beach

This roller-coaster stage gets off to a superb start, dropping in on the diminutive yet divine Mirtiotissas beach, 'perhaps the loveliest beach in the world', according to Lawrence Durrell. Sadly winter storms have drastically reduced the size but thankfully little of the charm of what is nowadays Corfu's unofficial nudist beach. Next comes a stiff climb over a panoramic saddle before a wander across the Ropa valley plain, flat as a pancake and ringed by modest hills. The day's conclusion is gorgeous if tiny Liapades beach, set among sheer cliffs. This is an especially long stage, and waymarking scarce on the ground. En route are several villages with cafés and facilities.

One way to shorten the day's load is an overnight stay at peaceful Kellia, or a little further on at Vatos. Another is to catch the bus from Kellia to Corfu Town and change there for the Liapades village run: then it's a 1.5km walk down the road to the beach.

From the square in **Pelekas** walk up to the crossroads near Jimmy's Restaurant and keep left around the yellow church. After the panoramically located Pink Panther restaurant a road forks left for Pelekas beach but the CT takes a descending concrete lane. Not far down it joins a minor road (left) and sticks with this past houses and rural properties to a junction. Here you leave the road (the left branch of which descends to Glifada beach), passing to the left of a building (Malibu Rooms). Hunt around for the yellow plaque on a tree pointing to a path left along

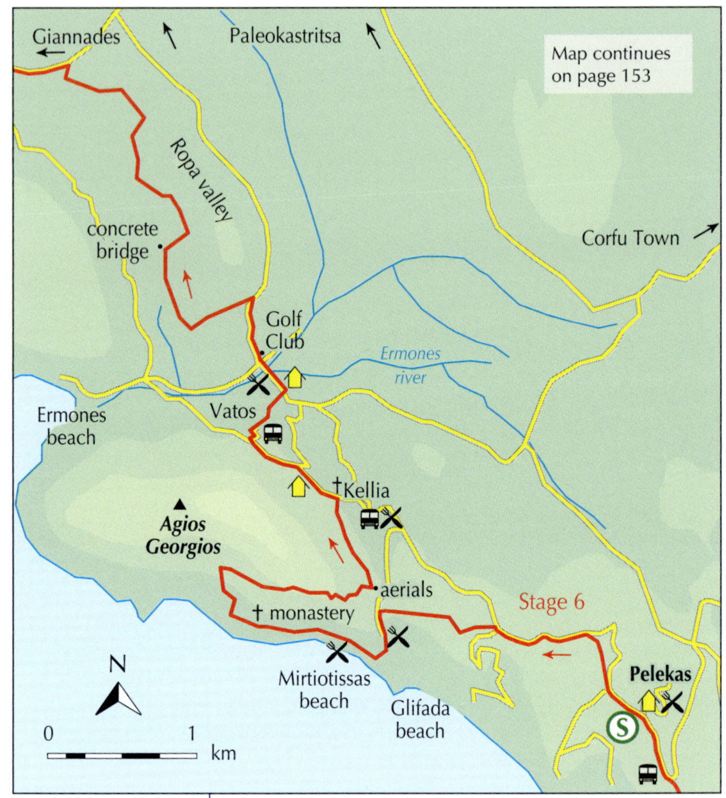

a fence. After a house it joins a lane left then at the ensuing fork goes right to continue NW through olive groves. Where it reaches a house, you turn downhill for a veritable plunge past a café-restaurant to the beautiful rocky bay housing **Mirtiotissas beach** (**50min**).

The way passes along the foot of awesome sheer cliffs where broom and even conifers somehow hang on, then climbs past the Bellavista taverna to the imposing gates of a well-kept **monastery**. Branch left past a bench and under the buildings on a path soon climbing through

olive groves. It's steadily uphill past derelict farm houses to a junction where a partially concreted lane is joined for a steep puff right (E). Time out to admire the brilliant views over the rugged coast eases the relentless ascent, as do pauses to appreciate the scented herbs that grow in abundance here. The lane cuts across the midriff of **Agios Georgios** mountain, whose summit is described in Walk 13.

The CT passes below the monastery at Mirtiotissas beach

A batch of **aerials** (200m) marks the point where the ridge is crossed. ▶ Not far over the other side, at a power pole, take the rough path right in descent through woodland. Down at a road, branch immediately left onto a lane W, soon a lovely path coasting through olive groves, above a rusting pick-up van. Bearing right (N) along a field, it emerges on the road near the pretty church at **Kellia** (**1hr 20min**, café and bus stop a short detour to the right).

The landscape opens up to include the east coast as well as the grassy Ropa valley spreading out north.

Follow the road left past houses and the alley to the Spiros Taverna (tel 26610 94309 mob 6932 701194

www.spirostaverna97.com for meals, groceries or accommodation). Continue through to the main road and head left past a **bus stop** to the square of **Vatos** (groceries). Follow markers carefully, soon right on an alley then a lane left downhill leaving houses behind. At animal pens a path breaks off, cutting down to join a road to an intersection near flats to let (Anastasia Apartments tel 26610 39416 mob 6972 773142). Turn left past a restaurant, café and grocery shop and proceed over the bridge past the **Golf Club**.

The main road bears left (for Ermones beach) but the CT continues straight on, crossing the grassy flat, bright with stands of yellow flags on the banks of channels. At the base of a knoll, branch left (in the opposite direction to the Theotoky Estate winery) onto a lane. ◄ Further along through trees, at a corner field with high chain-link fencing, branch right for a delightful stroll mostly N, through the flowered fields of the fertile **Ropa valley**. As you come to a **concrete bridge**, don't cross but instead turn right on a lane which soon peters out in a field – keep walking towards the base of the hill and at the trees bear left (NW). There are occasional yellow markings here. Along the edge of fields the shady lane passes olive groves, a farm and rows of cypresses. Keep left at the fork leading out to a road.

As the original CT is all but impossible to follow on the next section, turn left and follow the road the short way to an inviting **taverna** at a crossroads. Here follow the signs uphill to **Giannades** (150m, **1hr 30min**, café, shop) on its panoramic perch with vast views over the Ropa valley and its patchwork of fields. ◄

From the village square-cum-balcony, continue S. The road soon narrows to a paved alley between houses, bearing right to where tarmac takes over. Without going downhill, take the first fork right swinging NNW. Turn left at a nearby T-junction and continue gently uphill W, the road soon unsurfaced. As the way divides into two (about **15min** from Giannades) keep right, following an electricity line. Stick with the lane overlooking the Ropa valley. After the power lines end is a Y-junction where it's left on

Here is a lovely outlook back onto Agios Georgios mountain.

You are over halfway now.

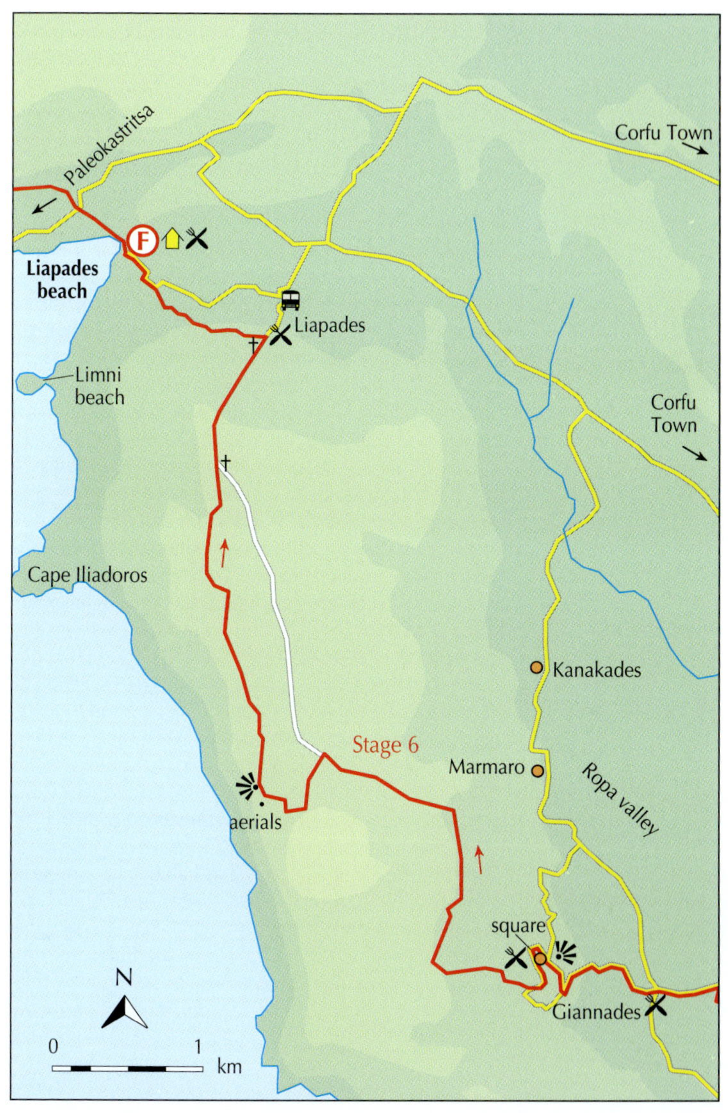

Corfu Town
Paleokastritsa
Liapades beach
Liapades
Limni beach
Cape Iliadoros
Corfu Town
Kanakades
Stage 6
Marmaro
Ropa valley
aerials
square
Giannades
N
0
1
km
F

a sunken lane. This is soon concreted and ascends NW a fern-filled valley to a minor road that you follow left uphill and across a crest through olive groves.

At a lane fork, swerve L in the direction of two **aerials**. As you near them and the lane starts to climb, branch right and through to wonderful **views** along Corfu's western coast. On a relaxing, level section known as the 'Olive Way' a never-ending sequence of groves now accompanies the CT on its way due N. For 3.5km you don't need to look out for elusive waymarks or turn-offs. A clearing spells views northwest to Paleokastritsa and soon afterwards you meet a road with a shrine. Go straight on, past a farm and downhill. At a fork with a concrete building it's left down to the paved alleys of **Liapades** village. Bear right down to the pretty shady square lined with cafés, eateries and a church (**2hr**).

The CT leaves the square alongside the church – stick with the narrow surfaced way dipping and climbing past buildings. At house n.491 fork right and downhill past olive trees. After a junction keep straight on then next right past apartments to where a stepped path breaks off right, down to the road. This leads towards **Liapades beach** (**20min**).

Before the bottom turn right for the Cricketer Taverna and Liapades Beach Hotel (tel 26630 41115 **www.liapades beachhotel.gr**) or continue down to the seafront and Elly Beach Hotel (tel 26630 41455).

Also known as Gefira beach, **Liapades beach** lies in a stunning bay surrounded by limestone cliffs. A refreshing dip is definitely on the cards!

Start	Liapades beach
Distance	11km
Ascent	320m
Descent	320m
Grade	2
Walking time	3hr 30min
Refreshments	Lakones, Krini, Agios Georgios north
Note	The final stretch between the Akrogiali Taverna and Agios Georgios north gets badly eroded by winter storms and can be muddy in spring, however it is bulldozed punctually at the start of every summer as a decent motorable track

A very lovely and not particularly tiring stage commencing with a climb to a belvedere village with extended views over the Paleokastritsa bay and rocky coastline. On and off stretches of tarmac lead to one of Corfu's best-preserved and scenic 'kalderimi', an old donkey track. The day concludes very satisfactorily at the long sandy beach of Agios Georgios north, set in a beautiful bay. Alternative accommodation is available en route, 2km after Lakones.

A tempting option that lengthens the stage by 1hr 30min goes to the ruins of the renowned Byzantine fortress of Angelokastro, set on a dramatic rock perch south of Krini.

At **Liapades beach** walk through the Elly Beach Hotel grounds and past the swimming pool. In the far corner of the garden yellow paint marks indicate the start of a stiff but short climb NW in thick wood below the awesome cliffs. Not far up is an easy short wooden **ladder** up a rock face. Down the other side at a concreted lane cross over, then bear right to buildings and the main Paleokastritsa road (supermarket, taverna, ATM and bus stop close by). ▶

Paleokastritsa itself is a further 3km west.

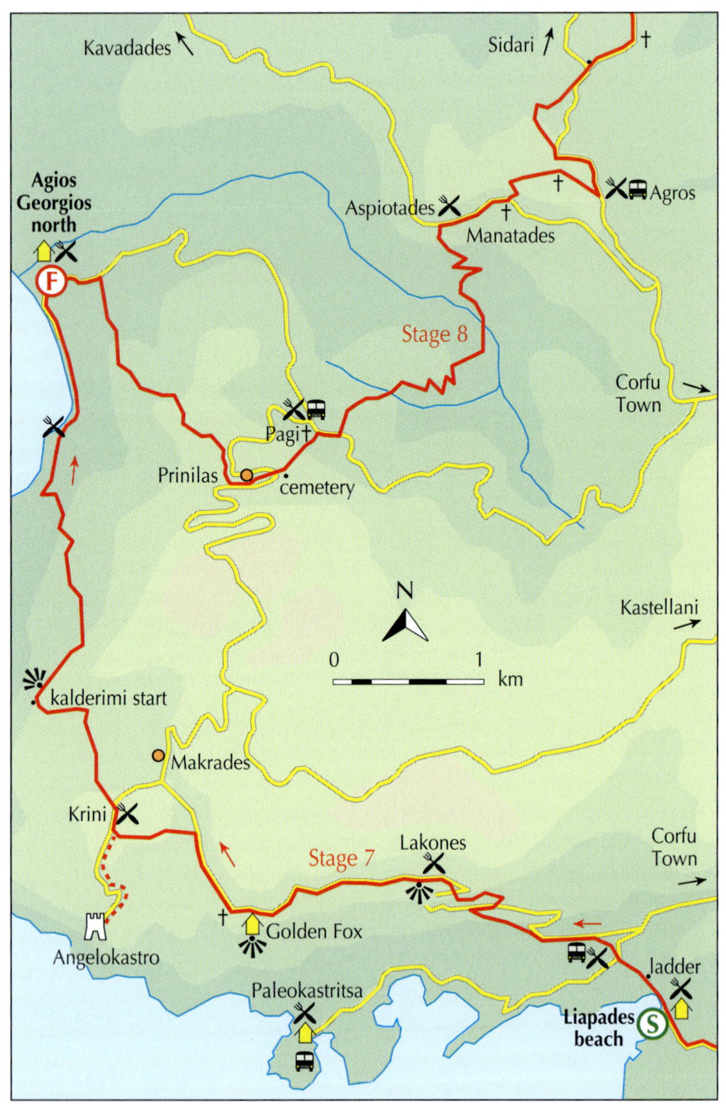

Kavadades
Sidari
Agios Georgios north
Aspiotades
Manatades
Agros
Stage 8
Corfu Town
Pagi
Prinilas
cemetery
N
0   1 km
Kastellani
kalderimi start
Makrades
Krini
Lakones
Stage 7
Corfu Town
Angelokastro
Golden Fox
Paleokastritsa
Liapades beach
ladder

On the other side of the road a concrete path leads along a fence up to the Lakones road. Follow this uphill (W) past Flavor Café to a corner where the CT branches left to pick up a signed path (right) for a shady climb through terraces of olive trees. As you approach the road again, go under the pedestrian tunnel then turn right – downhill. At the next bend, turn left up a concreted lane past a house to a signed fork left. This quickly becomes a beautiful old cobbled path with marvellous views. Cross a minor road and continue to climb on a rocky narrower way, slippery in places due to moss. This emerges to join tarmac for the final stretch up to belvedere par excellence **Lakones** (250m, **1hr 20min**). Stick with the panoramic road past cafés, a restaurant and a grocery shop, and through the village square. Further on belvedere café-restaurants that double as tour coach stops line the way, and souvenir stands are rife. You reach the **Golden Fox** with panoramic views of the bay (accommodation with special rates for walkers tel 26630 49101 **www.corfugoldenfox.com**).

Paleokastritsa can be admired from Lakones

Further on, after a **monastery** the road straightens, heading N. About halfway along this section (and **30min** from Lakones), before a sign for Makrades, take the lane off left (W). Narrowing to a path it bears left to join a dry stream bed. Keep an eye out for a path that soon climbs out right to meander W through olive groves. This widens to a lane in gentle ascent, before you leave it for another path (right) flanked by dry stone walls snaking its way through the olives. You emerge on a road.

Detour to Angelokastro

From here it is possible to detour left down the road to the base of **Angelokastro**. From the ticket booth a stiff but fascinating climb leads through the fortress' stone gateway arch. From the top the views are simply breathtaking over the beautiful coastline. A tiny chapel marks the highest point (305m), alongside curious dug-out graves. Allow **45min** for the walk each way. A modest entrance fee is charged.

The impressive fortress-cum-acropolis of **Angelokastro** dates back to the 1200s, the early Byzantine period. The name may derive from 'Angelo's castle', after a despot of Epirus who annexed the island to his region which now straddles Greece and Albania. It later fell into Venetian hands and became the governor's seat with a garrison. The castle occupies a strategic vantage point surveying the southern Adriatic and was a key lookout for shipping lanes, sending out warning signal fires to be relayed along the coast watchtowers to the fortresses at Corfu Town. Multi-storeyed, it had its own underground vaulted water cistern. Angelokastro played a leading part in repulsing Ottoman attacks in sieges from the 1500s to the 1700s.

If you don't take the detour, then go right to the tiny village square of **Krini** (300m, **40min**, shop, old-style café, drinking water, café-restaurant a short distance further along). Branch left here and along a paved alley. The CT takes the third right for a concrete lane down to traverse a valley where grapes grow in the shade of rock outcrops topped with a cross. Ignore the turn-off for Makrades and keep left. Soon you reach the start of the best bit, the spectacular and much photographed old **kalderimi** track. Through a section cut from the rock, you suddenly find yourself looking north over the magnificent bay of Agios Georgios and the Diapontian islands beyond. Edged with a low wall the way descends gently with hairpin bends NE beneath cliffs thick with wildflowers and broom. ▶

Watch your step towards the end as both the track and walls have collapsed in places.

Down at a concreted lane follow arrows L downhill. Mostly W it reaches a T-junction where you branch R for the gentle descent past the turn-off for the Fisherman's Cabin eatery. The glittering sea can continually be admired from the shady lane. Further along you reach the coast near the inviting Akrogiali fish **restaurant**. From here on you follow the seafront. Not far on is the beginning of the inviting sandy beach of **Agios Georgios north** (**1hr 30min**).

On the corner with the Ostrako Tavern, the road uphill leads to conveniently located seafront Alkyon Beach Hotel (tel 26630 96204 alkyonhotel@ymail.com). A short way further up are shops, cafés and Kostas Apartments, tel 26630 96337 **www.kostasapartments.gr**.

The paved streets of Krini

STAGE 8
Agios Georgios north to Sokraki

Start	Ostrako Tavern, Agios Georgios north
Distance	18km
Ascent	1000m
Descent	550m
Grade	2
Walking time	5hr 40min
Refreshments	Pagi, Aspiotades, Agros, Rekini, Valanio, Sokraki

Today the trail leaves the west coast behind to head eastwards inland through woodland, quiet villages and the inevitable lovely olive groves. A series of lanes and paths are followed on what is rather a tiring day as extra time may be needed for hunting around for elusive waymarks. The stage concludes at a tiny, peaceful mountain village in a lovely world of its own. A special spot.

If needs be, a handy exit point about halfway is Rekini, where the regular Roda–Corfu Town buses stop.

Leave the **Agios Georgios north** seafront at the Ostrako Tavern, by taking the road inland. After shops take the second fork right (almost opposite Angelos bar-restaurant). The tarmac soon runs out, and you pass a rusting bus. The ascent steepens and the way narrows, slippery in places due to the clay terrain. ◀ The path widens to a lane once more, and you keep straight ahead at forks. As yellow waymarks appear, the way bears L (E), levelling out and leading to a road. Go right twice and up a stepped alley past houses. At the next road turn left to soon traverse the tiny square of **Prinilas**. On the village outskirts take the lane along the left side of the **cemetery**, in descent NE. This leads to the imposing church of **Pagi** (260m, **1hr**).

At the foot of the bell tower go right (or left if you require cafés, shops or a bus). Then, where the road forks, keep left to a group of characteristic low stone buildings.

There's a fine outlook back over the bay.

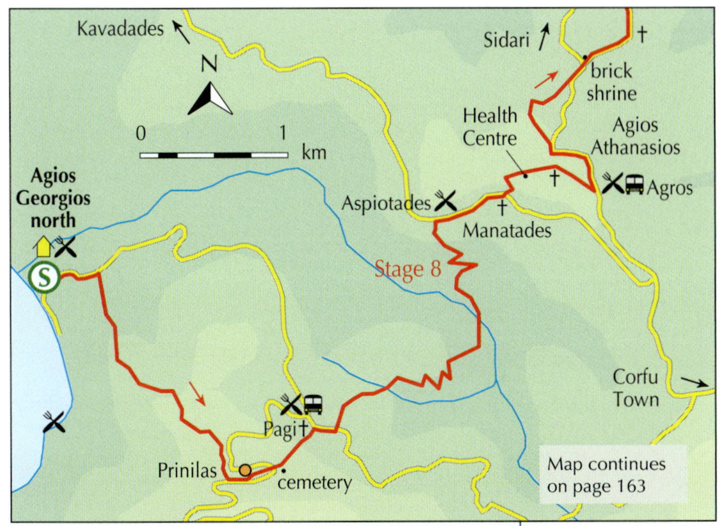

Soon the way veers right, passing an abandoned pick-up truck as you descend into a wooded valley with reeds and ferns and a stream. Continue NE to a shallow river which requires paddling across. Not far on join a road left past fields of potatoes and rusty sheds. At a modest house with a wire fence branch right on a broom-lined lane winding uphill. At tarmac go right for the final metres of ascent to a main road leading right past benches shaded by eucalyptus trees to the church and taverna of **Aspiotades**.

Stay on the road through neighbouring **Manatades**, and after its church the CT takes the 2nd left. ▶ Back on asphalt go right through olive groves to an intersection with aerials. Here fork right without entering the **Health Centre** premises, but keep left past Café P49 along the wall of a cemetery and down to a road, where you get views across to the Greek mainland. Here it's right to a curious church with numbers on its corner stones. Right at the next fork will see you at church-cum-belvedere, Agios Vasilios. A path through the flower beds descends on steps: don't miss the rusting torpedo on the left! Down

Cypress trees accompany the abruptly steep path.

The strategic junction and brick shrine out of Agios Athanasios

The ensuing section of the official CT detours left in a loop to avoid the main road. If preferred continue N for 1km along the tarmac to the brick shrine.

at houses stick with the main alley which emerges on the road at **Agros** (**1hr 20min**). Detour briefly right if you need a café, shop and bus stop.

Branch left through the neighbouring small village of Agios Athanasios. ◄ Fork left (sign for the Health Centre) then go next right up past houses. At a minor intersection keep straight ahead on a concrete-based lane among houses, then next left to a T-junction with a black railing. Here the CT turns right in gentle descent past grapevines, enjoying sweeping views. It's right at the next fork then straight over the ensuing crossroads, below a small car park. This drops through olive groves back to the main road, and it's not far to a fork with a **brick shrine**.

Branch right (NE) on the quiet road leading past a well-kept **monastery**. Some **10min** on, leave this for a lane left (NE) over a rise then down to cross the valley floor thick with tall reeds. It's a steady climb to a T-junction – turn right (SE) into shady olive groves and fenced properties, and over a bridge to finally reach the

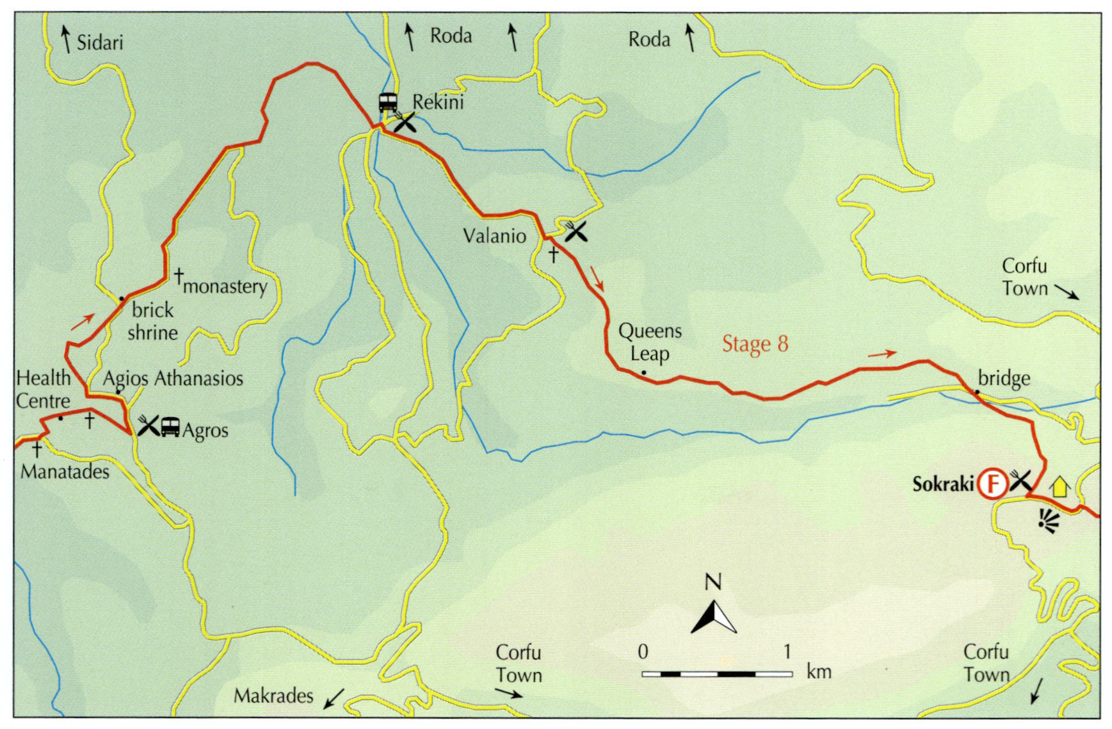

Sidari
Roda
Roda
Rekini
Valanio
monastery
brick shrine
Health Centre
Agios Athanasios
Agros
Manatades
Queens Leap
Stage 8
Corfu Town
bridge
Sokraki
F
N
Corfu Town
Makrades
Corfu Town
0
1
km

The original CT route is impassable from here to Valanio: instead follow these directions.

main road at **Rekini** (**1hr 20min**) and cafés. Go left across the river and past the bus stop on the bridge.

◀ At the busy intersection nearby, branch right near a clutch of signposts on a minor road climbing gently SSW past olive groves and cypresses. Entering the quiet village of **Valanio** (150m, **30min**) it passes a church. Turn left at the next junction: not far along, opposite a house smothered with roses, fork right under a Communist Party sign (otherwise straight ahead is a café and the village square). This soon leads along the left-hand flank of a graveyard and church, before ascending SE through olive groves thick with wild garlic, becoming an unsurfaced lane. At a fork the CT is pointed left downhill, and not far on it heads uphill again and to a board announcing the enigmatically named **Queens Leap**. Continue in the same direction on a level along a wide valley, whose flanks are cloaked in thick wood and its skyline lined with the dark green points of cypress trees.

Around **40min** from Queens Leap, cross a **bridge** and you're on tarmac, but not for long, as the CT branches right for a moss-ridden paved path SE. Through a path intersection with a circular well, continue gently uphill on an overgrown section with profuse ivy. This emerges on a grassy lane which leads left – the village of Sokraki finally comes into view, not far up now. You join a stony lane flanking fields planted with grape-vines, and soon bear right to climb the final metres to the tiny old village of **Sokraki** (440m, **1hr 30min**), positively buzzing with swallows but otherwise peaceful. It is beautifully located with vast **views** northeast to the bare limestone Pandokratoras massif.

Just to the right is the charming shady square, where two cafés serve refreshing drinks and simple fare.

Otherwise turn left down the road for Agallis Corfu Residence (tel 26630 2303 mob 6976 505642 **www. corfuvillage.com**). As an alternative, only 100m away (follow signs) is Sokraki Villas and Taverna (tel 26630 22176 **www.sokrakivillas.gr**).

STAGE 9
Sokraki to Old Perithia

Start	Sokraki square
Distance	13km
Ascent	600m
Descent	600m
Grade	2+
Walking time	5hr
Refreshments	Spartillas, Mount Pandokratoras, Old Perithia

The opening section of this splendid stage is a jaunt through a sun-blessed valley crammed with vineyards to the sleepy village of Spartillas. At this point the CT embarks on a tiring 600m ascent to cross Mount Pandokratoras, a rugged limestone massif and Corfu's highest elevation with dramatic stark landscapes – and splendid far-reaching panoramas, although the clutter of aerials on the top lessens its attractiveness. Fine settled weather is essential: low cloud can make orientation tricky, as both landmarks and waymarks are few and far between.

On the whole paths and waymarks are fairly good. The day concludes at the atmospheric, semi-abandoned village of Old Perithia (Paleá Períthia) on the mountain's northwestern flanks. Note that as accommodation in Old Perithia is limited (see below), two alternatives are suggested: either detour from Spartillas to attractive seafront Barbati, where there are more places to stay. Not an unpleasant option, as this entails a semi-rest day by a beach then a taxi back up next day. Otherwise be prepared for a double stage and proceed all the way to the CT conclusion – an additional 3hr 30min.

From **Sokraki** walk down the road past Agillas Corfu Residence to a bend in the road with a cement shed and shrine. Here the CT forks right (E) on a gently ascending lane that soon affords views southwest over the Ropa valley. At a fork, keep straight ahead on a rougher track descending through woodland. Soon a clear path takes over through a tunnel of woody bushes and along stone walls. Further on cross a lane and continue essentially in

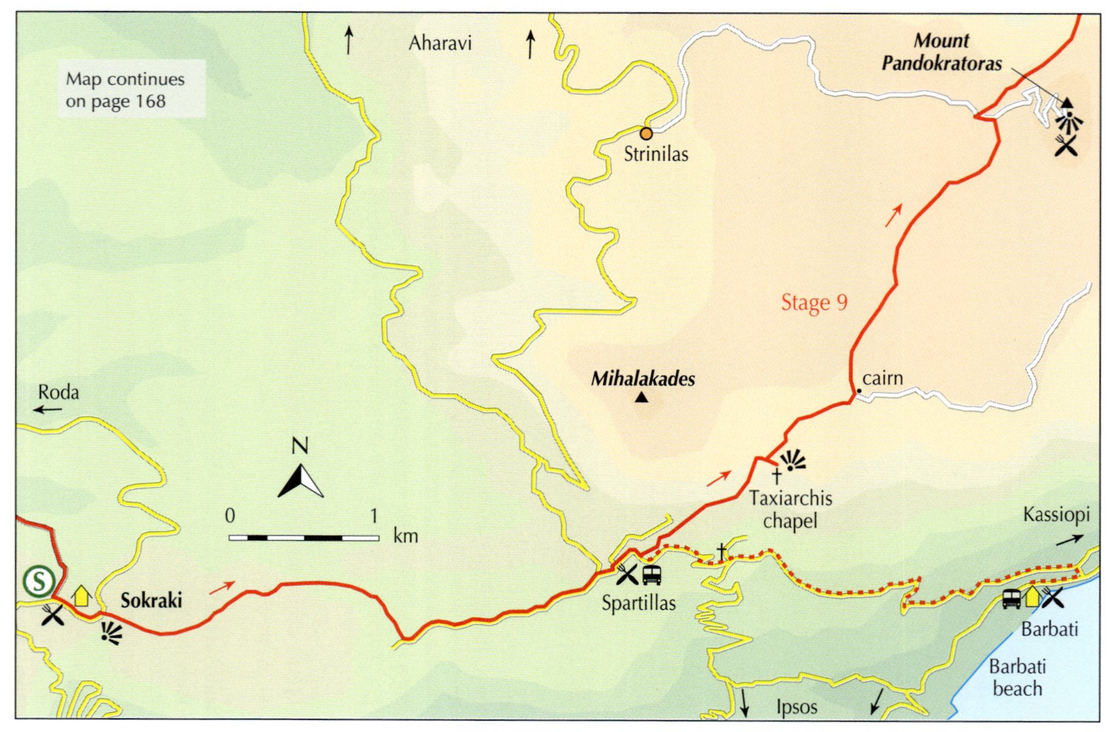

Aharavi
Map continues on page 168
Mount Pandokratoras
Strinilas
Stage 9
Mihalakades
cairn
Roda
N
Taxiarchis chapel
Kassiopi
0   1 km
Sokraki
Spartillas
Barbati
Barbati beach
Ipsos

Vineyards backed by Mount Pandokratoras on the way to Spartillas

the same direction, into a grassy clearing. Here a lane is joined downhill into a wood of dark green foliage: stick with this. ▶ At a T-junction keep left, soon on a tarmac surface through a beautiful, sheltered agricultural valley filled with flourishing vineyards dominated by the looming shape of Mount Pandokratoras. Further along you fork right on a main road to **Spartillas** (400m, **1hr 30min**, cafés, restaurants, groceries and the occasional bus), a laid-back village looking over the straits separating Corfu from the mainland.

Ignore yellow markings left for a narrow, slippery, overgrown clamber down abandoned stone terraces.

Detour to Barbati

Follow the panoramic road E downhill through the village. By all means shortcut the first two curves on clear stepped paths. At a bend with a shrine where two minor roads lead off, take the right-hand option. This drops steadily through shady olive groves to the main coast road and a bus stop. Go right into nearby **Barbati** (**1hr 15min**).

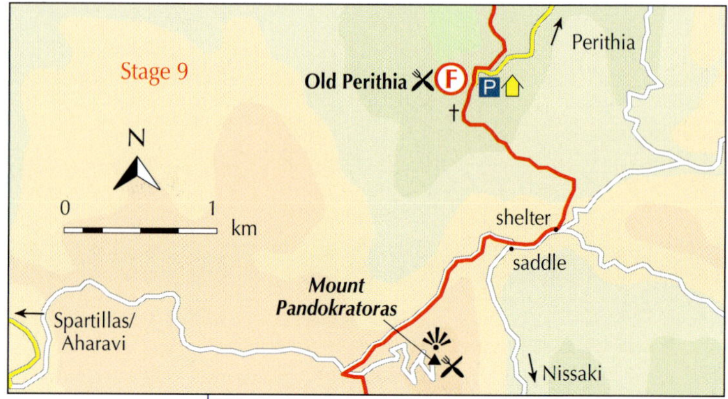

Barbati offers accommodation (such as Kiki's Apartments tel 26630 91176 email dorasi_17@hotmail.com), buses, tavernas, groceries and a pebble beach in a beautiful bay. Arrange for a taxi (tel 26610 30180) to deposit you back at Spartillas early next morning.

As you approach the centre of Spartillas, the road passes below the high retaining wall of a church before bearing right. At this point yellow paint splashes for the CT point you straight ahead off the tarmac for a paved way between old houses. Follow the markings carefully weaving through the maze of alleys to the rear of another church. Here it's sharp left up steps to a concreted lane past the last house of the village. After two rusting vehicles, continue on (NE) for a rougher lane traversing a mountainside thick with broom and shrubs. Don't miss the fork left for a path up through cultivated terraces giving way to flowering shrubs on a brilliantly panoramic stretch. Then it bears NNE up a damp valley where trees form a shady tunnel for walkers. Things open up again with low Mediterranean shrubs of heather and rock rose. At a cross and shoulder, the path levels out to a fork where you go R to the **Taxiarchis chapel** (650m, **45min**). ◄

Back at the fork, continue NNE in the direction of a communications tower. Ignore a turn-off for Strinilas

The tiny ruined building still boasts ancient frescoes, not to mention breathtaking views.

The rather featureless karst terrain on Mount Pandokratoras

and, dodging shrubs and rocks, walk on past goat pens and into damp mossy oak wood. Follow red markers gently uphill, concluding with a clamber over jagged rocks (watch your step) where you turn left (N) at a **cairn** onto a lane. Stick with this for about **10min** as far as a large bend left, where red and yellow arrows point you right. A path NNE on a red earth base crosses abandoned terraces on a gentle climb to the immense rugged karst plateau where desolate, featureless expanses are scattered with hardy plants and crisscrossed with the tracks of grazing livestock. All of a sudden the Pandokratoras summit itself – studded with aerials like a gigantic pin cushion – blasts into view. Follow the paint splashes meticulously in and out of a tiring series of karstic depressions, to finally emerge on the summit road (750m, **1hr 30min**) close to a rusty tank.

Time and energy permitting, you may like to detour the final 1.5km to the actual summit of **Mount**

Pandokratoras (911m) and a café, although the vast views on offer from the road are hardly bettered. Allow an extra **40min** return time.

Go left for a relaxing level stretch, and soon turn right onto the wide lane heading NE under the summit, the bare mountainsides home to skylarks and birds of prey. The way offers superb views to the Albanian coast, as well as the village of Old Perithia and even the trek conclusion at Agios Spiridonas far below. Imperceptible descent sees you curving past livestock pens to a **saddle** and fork. Ignore the branch right for Nissaki and keep straight on to a **shelter** at another fork.

Leave the lane for the clear path cutting N down the mountainside. Then at cairns and trees bear left down a way cleared through bracken. At the foot of a knoll a path bears W dipping across a valley and flowered slopes down to a lane. Turn left towards cypress trees and a **church** but branch right below the building and go right on a cobbled path snaking into peaceful, welcoming **Old Perithia** (420m, **1hr 15min**). At the first of the many tavernas, keep uphill to the car park.

The upmarket B&B The Merchant's House (tel 26630 98444 www.merchantshousecorfu.com) is the only place to overnight and usually imposes a two night minimum stay.

Old Perithia nestling in its valley, and the beckoning sea beyond

STAGE 10

Old Perithia to Agios Spiridonas

Start	Car park at Old Perithia
Distance	12km
Ascent	150m
Descent	550m
Grade	2
Walking time	3hr 30min
Refreshments	Almiros beach, Agios Spiridonas beach

This magnificent conclusion to the Corfu Trail initially follows the village of Old Perithia's ancient access way, plunging down a deep wooded valley to quiet hamlets. Follow route directions carefully, as waymarking is not especially abundant on this stretch.

At last down at the sea, the trail wanders along a beautiful sandy beach then the lovely rocky coast with secluded coves to Corfu's northernmost headland, before a fitting conclusion at Agios Spiridonas (sometimes spelt Agios Spyridon), named after the island's beloved patron saint. This northern coast is an inviting place to spend a couple of days to unwind.

From **Old Perithia** the CT takes the lane below the car park coasting initially N then bearing NNW. Where the lane ends a path continues in the same direction, descending through oak wood with ferns and accompanied by red/yellow arrows. Not far down all manner of flowering and scented shrubs encroach on an old way with stone edging descending the left side of a lovely gully-like valley, miles from anywhere, with promising glimpses of the glittering sea ahead. After a couple of wide curves, the gradient steepens as you enter shady dry woodland. A beautiful stretch ensues with relaxing bends down to cross bleached stones in the bed of the **Parigori river**, normally dry unless there has recently been a cloudburst. It climbs out the other side to resume the descent, finally emerging on a lane through olive groves.

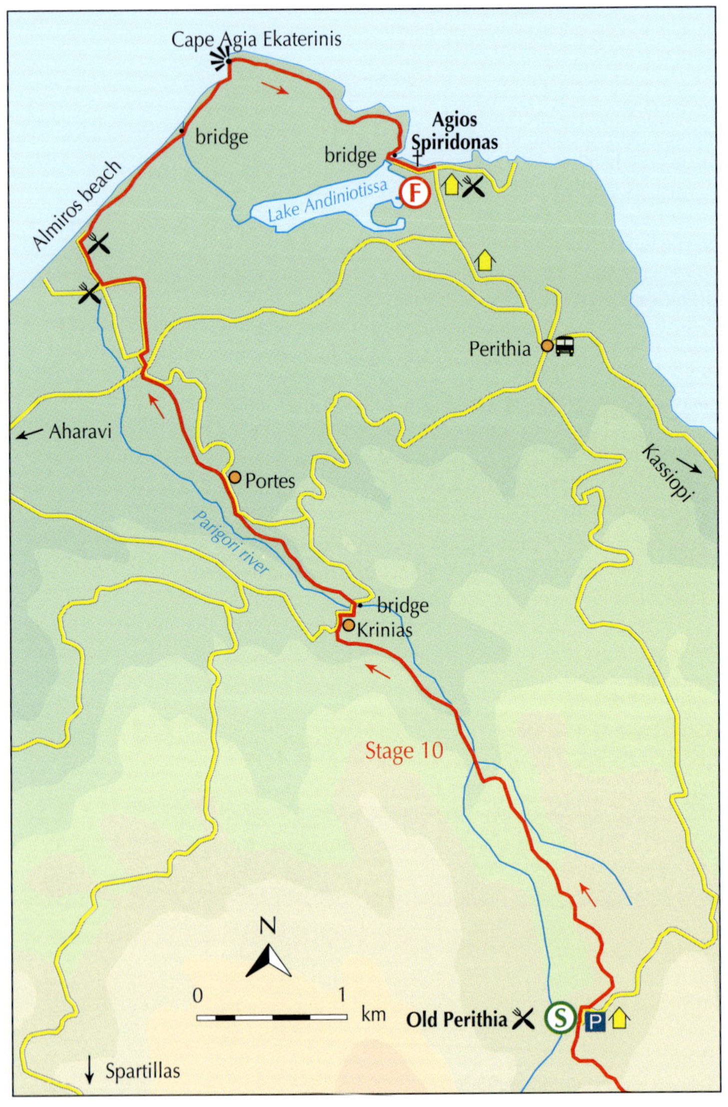

Cape Agia Ekaterinis
Agios Spiridonas
bridge
bridge
Almiros beach
Lake Andiniotissa
F
Perithia
Aharavi
Portes
Parigori river
Kassiopi
bridge
Krinias
Stage 10
N
0
1
km
Old Perithia
S
P
Spartillas

At a fork keep left over a rise to the handful of houses of **Krinias** (140m, **1hr 25min**).

Turn right (NE) down the road as far as a **bridge** then go left (NW) onto a lane. Where this concludes, a yellow marked path leads up to a concreted road leading left to the nearby hamlet of **Portes** (100m, **20min**).

As the roads forks out of the hamlet, the CT goes left on a gravel lane (sign for 'public footpath') between orchards. Soon becoming a path, it circles a fenced property and at the far corner you cross a lane for the path slightly uphill continuing NNW through olive groves. Yellow waymarking reappears and there are exciting views to the lake and coast that await. Across another lane you enter shady oak wood with brambles and emerge on a road. Left here will bring you out at the main coast road. Cross over with care and go right, but turn immediately left (sign for Almiros beach) on a side road lined with rows of tall eucalyptus trees. Take the next right, which quickly veers left towards the sea. At Taverna Zephyros fork right for the final run to inviting George Taverna and the glorious long white sandy expanse of **Almiros beach**, looking over to the mountains of Albania.

Continue NE parallel to the seafront and the last of the low dunes, to a **bridge**. This leads across a channel connected to nearby **Lake Andiniotissa** (out of sight here)

Cape Agia Ekaterinis, the northernmost point of Corfu

This is a stunning spot that marks the northernmost point of Corfu.

and onto what is actually an island. Keep on the lane along the coast to a pretty first beach, then take the red soil path across surprisingly jagged rocks to the white beacon tower on **Cape Agia Ekaterinis**. ◄ The path continues around the headland via a second beach. A little further on, as it reaches rocks, the way detours briefly inland through tall grass to a lane. Follow this to the right and soon left across another **bridge** over a lake outlet near fish traps and nets. This brings you to the lovely sandy expanse of **Agios Spiridonas** (**1hr 45min**) backed by shady eucalypts, a chapel and an inviting taverna.

A short distance along the seafront is the Mareblue Beach Resort (tel 26630 98500 **www.marebluebeachcorfu.com**) then more restaurants. Otherwise turn inland past the resort's main entrance to a supermarket at an intersection. Keep straight on past Karbouris Taverna to rooms at Villa Frangis (tel 26630 98329). A little further on is the main road – go left to the bus stop near the turn-off for Old Perithia.

The CT comes to a satisfying end at Agios Spiridion beach

The Kassiopi–Aharavi bus service along this stretch runs in summer. Otherwise Aharavi, 5km away, has the closest year-round service. The local taxi service is tel 26630 32400 **www.alfataxicorfu.net**.

APPENDIX A
Route summary tables

Day routes

Walk	Time	Distance	Ascent/Descent	Grade	Page
1 Kaminaki to Kerasia coastal path	3hr 30min	10.5km	50m/50m	1–2	34
2 Kalami to Menegoulas loop	5hr	15km	550m/550m	2–3	38
3 The Old Perithia trail	2hr 30min	9km	150m/550m	2	44
4 Around Cape Agia Ekaterinis	2hr	6km	negligible	1–2	48
5 The Panorama Trail above Aharavi	3hr 45min	12.5km	530m/530m	2	51
6 Cape Drastis	2hr 45min	10km	200m/200m	1–2	60
7 Agios Stefanos to Arillas	1hr 45min	5km	150m/150m	1–2	64
8 Porto Timoni	1hr 50min	3.5km	150m/150m	2	67
9 Fisherman's Cabin and the kalderimi	2hr 45min	8km	250m/250m	2	70
10 Paleokastritsa and Angelokastro loop	4hr	13km	600m/600m	2	73
11 Limni beach	1hr 40min	5.5km	150m/150m	1–2	78
12 Liniodoros beach	2hr 50min	8.5km	250m/250m	2	81
13 Mirtiotissas and Agios Georgios mountain	2hr 45min	7km	400m/400m	2	87
14 Agii Deka	2hr 15min	7.5km	300m/300m	2	90
15 Benitses to Dafnata	2hr 30min	7km	300m/300m	2	93
16 Agios Mattheos and Prasoudi	2hr 15min	5.5km	350m/350m	2	97

Walk	Time	Distance	Ascent/Descent	Grade	Page
17 Lake Korission circuit	4hr 30min	18km	negligible	1–2	104
18 Short Lake Korission route	3hr	11km	negligible	1	108
19 Chlomos loop	1hr 30min	4.5km	150m/150m	1–2	111
20 The Lefkimmi Salt Pans	2hr 15min	8.5km	negligible	1	115
21 Arkoudilas beach circuit	2hr 45min	9km	200m/200m	2	119
22 The Short Arkoudilas loop	2hr	7.5km	150m/150m	1–2	121

The Corfu Trail

Stage From/To	Time	Distance	Ascent/Descent	Grade	Page
1 Kavos/Potami	4hr 15min	14km	230m/230m	2	126
2 Potami/Agios Georgios sth	4hr 30min	15km	160m/160m	2	130
3 Agios Georgios sth/Paramonas	4hr 15min	15km	100m/80m	2	135
4 Paramonas/Dafnata	4hr 40min	14km	620m/340m	2	140
5 Dafnata/Pelekas	5hr 30min	17km	600m/700m	2	144
6 Pelekas/Liapades beach	6hr	22.5km	500m/700m	2	149
7 Liapades beach/Agios Georgios nth	3hr 30min	11km	320m/320m	2	155
8 Agios Georgios nth/Sokraki	5hr 40min	18km	1000m/550m	2	160
9 Sokraki/Old Perithia	5hr	13km	600m/600m	2+	165
10 Old Perithia/Agios Spiridonas	3hr 30min	12km	150m/550m	2	171

APPENDIX B
Accommodation

There is a huge choice of places to stay on Corfu; the following are suggestions.

Afionas
Panorama
tel 26630 51846
www.panoramacorfu.com

Porto Timoni
tel 26630 52051
www.portotimoni.gr

Agios Georgios north
Alkyon Beach Hotel
tel 26630 96204
alkyonhotel@ymail.com

Kostas Apartments
tel 26630 96337
www.kostasapartments.gr

Pension Vrachos
tel 26630 51323
www.vrachospension.com

Agios Georgios south
Barbayannis
tel 26620 52110

Blue Sea Hotel
tel 26620 51624
www.bluesea-hotel.com

Agios Spiridonas
Mareblue Beach Resort (reasonably priced in low season)
tel 26630 98500
www.marebluebeachcorfu.com

Villa Frangis
tel 26630 98329

Aharavi
Marie Hotel
tel 26630 63108
www.mariehotelcorfu.com

Alonaki Bay
Alonaki Beach Taverna
tel 26610 75872

Arillas
Hotel Horizon
tel 26630 51780
www.horizon-hotel.gr

Benitses
Argo Taverna and Rooms
tel 26610 72630
http://argobenitses.gr

Hotel Riviera
tel 26610 72004
www.corfuriviera.gr

Chlomos
Balis Taverna
tel 26620 52449
mob 6948 271216
www.corfu-balis.gr

Corfu Town
City Marina
tel 26610 39505
www.citymarina.gr

Hotel Atlantis
tel 26610 35560
www.atlantis-hotel-corfu.com

Kalami

Lena Garnelli Apartments
tel 26630 91744
mob 6932 869853
www.lenagarnelliapartments.gr

The White House
tel 26630 91040
www.corfu-kalami.gr

Lakonas

Golden Fox (2km from the village,
special rates for walkers)
tel 26630 49101
www.corfugoldenfox.com

Liapades Beach

Elly Beach Hotel
tel 26630 41455

Liapades Beach Hotel
tel 26630 41115
www.liapadesbeachhotel.gr

Nissaki Bay

Nissaki Bay Apartments
tel 26630 91455
www.nissakibay.gr

Old Perithia

The Merchant's House B&B (upmarket)
tel 26630 98444
www.merchantshousecorfu.com

Paleokastritsa

Apollon Hotel
tel 26630 41211
www.corfu-apollon-hotel.com

Zefiros Hotel
tel 26630 41244
www.zefiroscorfuhotel.gr

Paramonas

Paramonas Hotel
tel 26610 76595
www.paramonas-hotel.com

Rooms Varagulis Giannis
tel 26610 76702

Pelekas

Agnes Rooms
tel 26610 94997
www.agnespelekas.com

Jimmy's Restaurant and Rooms
tel 26610 94284
mob 6973 596644
www.jimmyspelekas.com

Sidari

Mimosa Hotel
tel 26630 95363
www.hotelmimosacorfu.com

Sokraki

Agallis Corfu Residence
tel 26630 2303
mob 6976 505642
www.corfuvillage.com

Sokraki Villas and Taverna
(1.5km out of the village)
tel 26630 22176
www.sokrakivillas.gr

Accommodation for the Corfu Trail

Kavos

Rantos Apartments B&B
tel 26620 61361
mob 6948 572957
www.rantosapartments.com

San Marina Hotel
tel 26620 61345
www.corfusanmarina.com

Potami (Lefkimmi)
The River Restaurant
tel 26620 24032
mob 6974 613677

Rooms to let
mob 6945 973779

Gardenos
Alexandros Taverna
mob 6976 215429

Santa Barbara
Maria Rooms
tel 26620 23151
www.corfusantabarbara.com

Agios Georgios south
Barbayannis
tel 26620 52110

Blue Sea Hotel
tel 26620 51624
www.bluesea-hotel.com

Paramonas
Paramonas Hotel
tel 26610 76595
www.paramonas-hotel.com

Rooms Varagulis Giannis
tel 26610 76702

Dafnata
Kostas Raris Taverna and Rooms
tel 26610 57345
mob 6946 471449
kosraris@yahoo.gr

The Olive Press
tel 26610 57307

Pelekas
Agnes Rooms
tel 26610 94997
www.agnespelekas.com

Jimmy's Restaurant and Rooms
tel 26610 94284
mob 6973 596644
www.jimmyspelekas.com

Kellia
Spiros Taverna
tel 26610 94309
mob 6932 701194
www.spirostaverna97.com

Vatos
Anastasia Apartments
tel 26610 39416
mob 6972 773142

Liapades Beach
Elly Beach Hotel
tel 26630 41455

Liapades Beach Hotel
tel 26630 41115
www.liapadesbeachhotel.gr

2km after Lakones
Golden Fox (special rates for walkers)
tel 26630 49101
www.corfugoldenfox.com

Agios Georgios north
Alkyon Beach Hotel
tel 26630 96204
alkyonhotel@ymail.com

Kostas Apartments
tel 26630 96337
www.kostasapartments.gr

Sokraki

Agallis Corfu Residence
tel 26630 2303
mob 6976 505642
www.corfuvillage.com

Sokraki Villas and Taverna
(1.5km out of the village)
tel 26630 22176
www.sokrakivillas.gr

Barbati

Kiki's Apartments
tel 26630 91176
email dorasi_17@hotmail.com

Old Perithia

The Merchant's House B&B (upmarket)
tel 26630 98444
www.merchantshousecorfu.com

Agios Spiridonas

Mareblue Beach Resort
(reasonably priced in low season)
tel 26630 98500
www.marebluebeachcorfu.com

Villa Frangis
tel 26630 98329

Gorgeous outlook over Porto Timoni (Walk 8)

APPENDIX C
English–Greek glossary and expressions

A handful of terms found on maps and signs. These are transcriptions from the Greek characters, so variations in spelling are inevitable.

agia	female saint	*moni*	monastery
agios	male saint	*nisos*	island
akrotiri	cape, headland	*ormos*	wide bay
eklisia	church	*oros*	mountain
kalderimi	donkey track	*paralia*	beach, coast
kilada	valley	*pelagos*	sea
kolpos	narrow bay	*potami*	river
limni	lake, lagoon		

Useful expressions

NB 'h' is pronounced as in 'loch'

yes	*ne*	good evening (6–10pm)	*kalo vrathi*
no	*o-hi*	good night	*kali nikta*
OK	*entaxi*	how much is it?	*posokani?*
thank you	*efharisto*	the bill	*loghariazmos*
please/ you're welcome	*parakalo*	where is ...?	*pou ine ...?*
cheers!	*yammas!*	bread	*psomi*
hello	*ya sas*	cheese	*tyri*
good morning	*kali mera*	coffee	*cafe*
good afternoon (2–6pm)	*kali spera*	ham	*choiromeri*
		tea	*chai*

APPENDIX D
Further reading

Recommended reading is the hilarious Gerald Durrell 1956 classic *My Family and Other Animals*, as well as his elder brother Lawrence Durrell's *Prospero's Cell* (1945). Jan Morris' *The Venetian Empire* (1980) and JJ Norwich's *The Middle Sea* (2007) are informative background reading.

Wildflower enthusiasts will appreciate *Wild Flowers of the Mediterranean* by Marjorie Blamey and Christopher Grey-Wilson as well as *Flowers of the Mediterranean* by Oleg Polunin and Anthony Huxley.

A light-hearted account of the Corfu Trail is John Waller's *Walking the Corfu Trail* (2010).

Spring wildflowers on Almiros beach (Walk 3)

NOTES

NOTES

NOTES

NOTES

NOTES

NOTES

LISTING OF CICERONE GUIDES

BRITISH ISLES CHALLENGES, COLLECTIONS AND ACTIVITIES
Great Walks on the England Coast Path
Map and Compass
The Big Rounds
The Book of the Bivvy
The Book of the Bothy
The Mountains of England and Wales:
Vol 1 Wales
Vol 2 England
The National Trails
Walking the End to End Trail

SHORT WALKS SERIES
Short Walks Hadrian's Wall
Short Walks in the Lake District:
Keswick, Borrowdale and Buttermere
Short Walks in the Lake District:
Windermere Ambleside and Grasmere
Short Walks in the Lake District:
Coniston and Langdale
Short Walks in Arnside and Silverdale
Short Walks in Nidderdale
Short Walks in Northumberland:
Wooler, Rothbury, Alnwick and the coast
Short Walks on the Malvern Hills
Short Walks in Cornwall:
Falmouth and the Lizard
Short Walks in Cornwall:
Land's End and Penzance
Short Walks in the South Downs:
Brighton, Eastbourne and Arundel
Short Walks in the Surrey Hills
Short Walks Winchester
Short Walks in Pembrokeshire:
Tenby and the south
Short Walks on the Isle of Mull
Short Walks on the Orkney Islands

SCOTLAND
Ben Nevis and Glen Coe
Cycling in the Hebrides
Cycling the North Coast 500
Great Mountain Days in Scotland
Mountain Biking in Southern and Central Scotland
Mountain Biking in West and North West Scotland
Not the West Highland Way Scotland
Scotland's Best Small Mountains
Scotland's Mountain Ridges
Scottish Wild Country Backpacking
Short Walks in Dumfries and Galloway
Skye's Cuillin Ridge Traverse
The Borders Abbeys Way
The Great Glen Way

The Great Glen Way Map Booklet
The Hebridean Way
The Hebrides
The Isle of Mull
The Isle of Skye
The Skye Trail
The Southern Upland Way
The West Highland Way
West Highland Way Map Booklet
Walking Ben Lawers, Rannoch and Atholl
Walking in the Cairngorms
Walking in the Pentland Hills
Walking in the Scottish Borders
Walking in the Southern Uplands
Walking in Torridon, Fisherfield, Fannichs and An Teallach
Walking Loch Lomond and the Trossachs
Walking on Arran
Walking on Harris and Lewis
Walking on Jura, Islay and Colonsay
Walking on Rum and the Small Isles
Walking on the Orkney and Shetland Isles
Walking on Uist and Barra
Walking the Cape Wrath Trail
Walking the Corbetts
Vol 1 South of the Great Glen
Vol 2 North of the Great Glen
Walking the Galloway Hills
Walking the John o' Groats Trail
Walking the Munros
Vol 1 — Southern, Central and Western Highlands
Vol 2 — Northern Highlands and the Cairngorms
Winter Climbs in the Cairngorms
Winter Climbs: Ben Nevis and Glen Coe

NORTHERN ENGLAND ROUTES
Cycling the Reivers Route
Cycling the Way of the Roses
Hadrian's Cycleway
Hadrian's Wall Path
Hadrian's Wall Path Map Booklet
Pennine Way Map Booklet
The Coast to Coast Cycle Route
The Coast to Coast Walk
The Coast to Coast Map Booklet
The Pennine Way
Walking the Dales Way
The Dales Way Map Booklet

LAKE DISTRICT
Bikepacking in the Lake District
Cycling in the Lake District
Great Mountain Days in the Lake District
Joss Naylor's Lakes, Meres and Waters of the Lake District

Lake District Winter Climbs
Lake District:
High Level and Fell Walks
Low Level and Lake Walks
Mountain Biking in the Lake District
Outdoor Adventures with Children — Lake District
Scrambles in the Lake District —
North
South
Trail and Fell Running in the Lake District
Walking The Cumbria Way
Walking the Lake District Fells —
Borrowdale
Buttermere
Coniston
Keswick
Langdale
Mardale and the Far East
Patterdale
Wasdale
Walking the Tour of the Lake District

NORTH—WEST ENGLAND AND THE ISLE OF MAN
Cycling the Pennine Bridleway
Isle of Man Coastal Path
The Lancashire Cycleway
The Lune Valley and Howgills
Walking in Cumbria's Eden Valley
Walking in Lancashire
Walking in the Forest of Bowland and Pendle
Walking on the Isle of Man
Walking on the West Pennine Moors
Walking the Ribble Way
Walks in Silverdale and Arnside

NORTH—EAST ENGLAND, YORKSHIRE DALES AND PENNINES
Cycling in the Yorkshire Dales
Great Mountain Days in the Pennines
Mountain Biking in the Yorkshire Dales
The Cleveland Way and the Yorkshire Wolds Way
The Cleveland Way Map Booklet
The North York Moors
Trail and Fell Running in the Yorkshire Dales
Walking in County Durham
Walking in Northumberland
Walking in the North Pennines
Walking in the Yorkshire Dales:
North and East
South and West
Walking St Cuthbert's Way
Walking St Oswald's Way and Northumberland Coast Path

Walking on Madeira
Walking on the Azores

SWITZERLAND
Switzerland's Jura Crest Trail
The Swiss Alps
Tour of the Jungfrau Region
Trekking the Swiss Via Alpina
Walking in Arolla and Zinal
Walking in the Bernese Oberland
    — Jungfrau region
Walking in the Engadine —
    Switzerland
Walking in the Valais
Walking in Ticino
Walking in Zermatt and Saas—Fee

GERMANY
Hiking and Cycling in the
    Black Forest
The Danube Cycleway Vol 1
The Rhine Cycle Route
The Westweg
Walking in the Bavarian Alps

**POLAND, SLOVAKIA,
ROMANIA, HUNGARY AND
BULGARIA**
The Danube Cycleway Vol 2
The High Tatras
The Mountains of Romania

**SCANDINAVIA, ICELAND AND
GREENLAND**
Hiking in Norway — South
Trekking the Kungsleden
Trekking in Greenland — The
    Arctic Circle Trail
Walking and Trekking in Iceland

**SLOVENIA, CROATIA, SERBIA,
MONTENEGRO AND ALBANIA**
Hiking Slovenia's Juliana Trail
Mountain Biking in Slovenia
The Islands of Croatia
The Julian Alps of Slovenia
The Mountains of Montenegro
The Peaks of the Balkans Trail
The Slovene Mountain Trail
Walking in Slovenia:
    The Karavanke
Walks and Treks in Croatia

ITALY
Alta Via 1 — Trekking in the
    Dolomites
Alta Via 2 — Trekking in the
    Dolomites
Day Walks in the Dolomites
Italy's Grande Traversata delle Alpi
Italy's Sibillini National Park
Ski Touring and Snowshoeing in
    the Dolomites
The Way of St Francis
Trekking Gran Paradiso: Alta Via 2
Trekking in the Apennines

Trekking the Giants' Trail:
    Alta Via 1 through the Italian
    Pennine Alps
Via Ferratas of the Italian Dolomites
    Vol 1
    Vol 2
Walking in Abruzzo
Walking in Italy's Cinque Terre
Walking in Italy's Stelvio National
    Park
Walking in Sicily
Walking in the Aosta Valley
Walking in the Dolomites
Walking in Tuscany
Walking in Umbria
Walking Lake Como and Maggiore
Walking Lake Garda and Iseo
Walking on the Amalfi Coast
Walks and Treks in the Maritime Alps

IRELAND
The Wild Atlantic Way and
    Western Ireland
Walking the Kerry Way
Walking the Wicklow Way

EUROPEAN CYCLING
Cycling the Route des Grandes Alpes
Cycling the Ruta Via de la Plata
The Elbe Cycle Route
The River Loire Cycle Route
The River Rhone Cycle Route

**INTERNATIONAL CHALLENGES,
COLLECTIONS AND ACTIVITIES**
Europe's High Points
Walking the Via Francigena
    Pilgrim Route —
    Part 1
    Part 2
    Part 3

AUSTRIA
Innsbruck Mountain Adventures
Trekking Austria's Adlerweg
Trekking in Austria's Hohe Tauern
Trekking in Austria's Zillertal Alps
Trekking in the Stubai Alps
Walking in Austria
Walking in the Salzkammergut:
    the Austrian Lake District

MEDITERRANEAN
The High Mountains of Crete
Trekking in Greece
Walking and Trekking in Zagori
Walking and Trekking on Corfu
Walking on the Greek Islands —
    the Cyclades
Walking in Cyprus
Walking on Malta

HIMALAYA
8000 metres
Everest: A Trekker's Guide
Trekking in the Karakoram

NORTH AMERICA
Hiking and Cycling the California
    Missions Trail
The John Muir Trail
The Pacific Crest Trail

SOUTH AMERICA
Aconcagua and the Southern Andes
Hiking and Biking Peru's Inca Trails
Trekking in Torres del Paine

AFRICA
Kilimanjaro
Walking in the Drakensberg
Walks and Scrambles in the
    Moroccan Anti-Atlas

**NEW ZEALAND AND
AUSTRALIA**
Hiking the Overland Track

CHINA, JAPAN, AND ASIA
Annapurna
Hiking and Trekking in the Japan
    Alps and Mount Fuji
Hiking in Hong Kong
Japan's Kumano Kodo Pilgrimage
Trekking in Bhutan
Trekking in Ladakh
Trekking in Tajikistan
Trekking in the Himalaya

TECHNIQUES
Fastpacking
The Mountain Hut Book

MINI GUIDES
Alpine Flowers
Navigation
Pocket First Aid and
    Wilderness Medicine
Snow

MOUNTAIN LITERATURE
A Walk in the Clouds
Abode of the Gods
Fifty Years of Adventure
The Pennine Way —
    the Path, the People, the Journey
Unjustifiable Risk?

For full information on all our
guides, books and eBooks,
visit our website:
www.cicerone.co.uk

CICERONE

Trust Cicerone to guide your next adventure,
wherever it may be around the world...

Discover guides for hiking, mountain walking, backpacking, trekking, trail running, cycling and mountain biking, ski touring, climbing and scrambling in Britain, Europe and worldwide.

Connect with Cicerone online and find inspiration.

- buy books and ebooks
- articles, advice and trip reports
- podcasts and live events
- GPX files and updates
- regular newsletter

cicerone.co.uk